FOR AS LONG AS WE BOTH SHALL LIVE

 ROGER FRITTS

AVON BOOKS ◆ NEW YORK

Copyrights protect most of the selections in this volume. Because this page cannot fit all copyright notices, the section in the back of the book designated "Acknowledgments" is an extension of this copyright page. When no name appears following a selection, Roger Fritts is the author.

FOR AS LONG AS WE BOTH SHALL LIVE is an original publication of Avon Books. This work has never before appeared in book form.

AVON BOOKS
A division of
The Hearst Corporation
1350 Avenue of the Americas
New York, New York 10019

First Avon Books Trade Printing: September 1993

AVON TRADEMARK REG. U.S. PAT. OFF. AND IN OTHER COUNTRIES, MARCA REGISTRADA, HECHO EN U.S.A.

Printed in the U.S.A.

ARC   10   9   8   7   6   5   4

Contents

Contents

Contents

Contents

Introduction

I officiated at my first wedding when I was twenty-four. It was a stressful moment in my ministry.

WE ARE GATHERED AT THIS HOUR TO WITNESS AND TO CELEBRATE THE MARRIAGE OF TWO SEPARATE LIVES . . .

One of my legs began to tremble.

INTO THIS RELATIONSHIP WITH DEEP COMMITMENT AND HIGH EXPECTATION THESE TWO COME TO JOIN THEMSELVES . . .

My leg trembled more. I wondered if my robe was shaking. I spoke faster.

WILL YOU HAVE THIS MAN TO BE YOUR HUSBAND, TO LOVE AND TO CHERISH, TO HONOR AND TO COMFORT, IN SICKNESS OR IN HEALTH, IN SORROW OR IN JOY . . .

"Relax," I said silently to my nervous body. A vision came to me of how I would look when my legs gave way from tension and I found myself kneeling before the couple.

INASMUCH AS YOU HAVE CONSENTED TOGETHER IN MARRIAGE, I PRONOUNCE YOU HUSBAND AND WIFE . . .

The mother of the bride cried. I wondered if she had seen my shaking legs. After the service I offered my congratulations, signed the license and headed for my office.

As I look back now on this experience, I suspect my anxiety flowed partly from my image of a "perfect" wedding. It is a common image derived from television, movies, magazines and books. The site is a beautiful old church. The bride dresses in an elaborate white wedding gown. The groom

wears a black tuxedo. There are bridesmaids, a best man, a flower girl and several other attendants. The minister is a wise, calm, white-haired male.

Since that first wedding, I have learned that weddings do not all need to strive for the same goal to be deeply meaningful. There are many ways to get married. The couples I work with have taught me about the variety of this religious ritual. Weddings can be outside or inside. A couple can write their own service or they can follow a traditional text. The service can be humorous or serious. It can be big or small. It can be formal or informal. This discovery lifted a great weight of anxiety from my shoulders. My legs no longer shook in fear.

Because our society supports freedom of religion, we do not need to conform to someone's expectations of the perfect wedding. We can support each other in our right to make our own decisions about this religious celebration. There is no one "perfect" wedding. There are thousands of splendid, unique weddings.

A wedding is a hinge in time, an event that marks our passage from one major stage of our lives to a new stage. It is an important day in our lives, equal to such events as the birth of a child or the death of someone close. However, unlike births and deaths, with weddings we can control the time, the place and the circumstances of the event. The process of planning a wedding can result in considerable joy and considerable anxiety. I hope this book will help you in this process. It is the result of helping over one thousand couples prepare their own wedding services.

After reading these pages you may decide to select a traditional wedding service from the appendices, or you may decide to write your own service. I invite you to use this book freely to design a service that reflects your values, beliefs and tastes. Whatever you decide about your service, having reviewed the alternatives, you can make your decision understanding the reason for each part of the wedding ceremony.

The Organization of This Book

The heart of this book is a comparison between the basic elements of the Protestant, Roman Catholic and Jewish services.

For the example of a Protestant wedding service I have used the 1979 *Book of Common Prayer*. This is the wedding service of the Protestant Episcopal Church of the United States. Each American Protestant denomination has its own wedding liturgy. However, most Protestant services are indebted to the *Book of Common Prayer* wedding ceremony for their general structure and for some or much of their content.

Thomas Cranmer prepared the first *Book of Common Prayer* in 1549. It was radically revised in 1552 and received minor revisions in 1559, 1604 and 1662. A central motivation of the English decision to break away from the Roman Catholic Church was the English king's desire to have the freedom to divorce and remarry. Thus, the wedding service was a central part of the responsibilities of the Anglican Church. In contrast, other early Protestants rejected responsibility for weddings. German and Swiss leaders of the Protestant Reformation did not see officiating at wedding services as the duty of the clergy. Luther advised clergy to leave the weddings to lawyers and judges. Calvin thought religion was no more involved in marriage than in "agriculture, architecture, shoe making, and many other things." However, British institutions have had a strong, central influence on American culture. Consequently, today churches in the United States that trace their heritage back to Luther or Calvin have disregarded their founders' dismissal of church weddings. Most American Protestant churches have adopted the Episcopal view that wedding services are an important part of the church's responsibility.

The 1662 *Book of Common Prayer* continued as standard liturgy for Anglican Churches until the 1970s. In the twentieth century, priests developed experimental liturgies with contemporary language, dropping Old English words such as "troth" and changing "wilt thou" to "will you." After much controversy, the Church of England and the Protestant Episcopal Church in the United States fully adopted this contemporary language at the end of the 1970s. This is the version that appears in these pages.

The Roman Catholic service used in this book first appeared in 1969 and

is a result of the Second Vatican Council (1962–65). This council overturned the traditional use of Latin as the sole liturgical language. It prescribed the use of everyday language for liturgies and ordered the reform of all sacramental rites, such as the wedding rite. During the twentieth century the Roman Catholic Church in the United States has greatly relaxed its rules regarding interfaith marriages. Today the primary requirement is that the Catholic in the marriage promise to have his or her children baptized and raised as Catholics.

The Jewish religious community in the United States is divided into three major groups. Orthodox Judaism is the religion of those Jews that adhere most strictly to traditional beliefs and practices. In the United States many Orthodox synagogues have joined to form The Union of Orthodox Jewish Congregations of America. In the State of Israel, Orthodoxy is the official form of Judaism. Conservative Judaism seeks to conserve essential elements of traditional Judaism but allows for modernization of religious practices. In the United States the United Synagogue of America represents the Conservative movement. Reform Judaism has modified or abandoned many traditional Jewish beliefs, laws and practices to adapt Judaism to the changing social, political and cultural conditions of today. It is organized as the Union of American Hebrew Congregations and the Central Conference of American Rabbis. The Jewish wedding service in this book is from Reform Judaism. It is from the *Rabbi's Manual* published in 1988 by the Central Conference of American Rabbis. All three Jewish groups oppose intermarriage of Jews with non-Jews. They argue that when a husband and wife disagree on an issue as basic as their religion, it harms the prospect for a lasting and harmonious relationship. However, some Reform rabbis will officiate at interfaith marriages.

In planning this anthology of wedding services I came to the conclusion that there is value in having each chapter show one part of a wedding service. I also believe that there is value in showing complete services from beginning to end.

The value of the first structure is that the reader can easily compare the different ways various religious traditions handle such things as the exchange of vows or the pronouncement. In my experience, few people pick up a book like this looking for a wedding service they will use from beginning to end for their wedding. Instead, most people will create their own

service. The couple will pick a ring ceremony from one writer. They will pick vows from another writer. They will change words here and there, and they will write some words themselves. In this way they will arrive at a wedding service that reflects their tastes, personalities and relationship. I have designed the first chapters of this book to help you in this process. Here are the basic parts of a traditional American wedding service:

THE OPENING WORDS are a brief statement about the meaning and value of love and marriage.

THE READINGS, from the Bible or another source, affirm and support the opening statement about love and marriage.

THE QUESTION OF INTENT asks the couple to promise the community that they will create a stable, lasting marriage.

THE VOWS are the promises the couple make to each other.

THE RINGS are blessed by the cleric and exchanged as symbols of the promises made in the vows.

THE BLESSING is a request by the cleric to God, asking God's support for the marriage.

THE ANNOUNCEMENT OR DECLARATION is a summary and affirmation of what has just occurred.

THE CLOSING WORDS are a statement of hope for the future.

There are limits to the process of breaking down wedding services into their individual elements. Most wedding services, when they are finished, work as a whole, with an intentional theme, structure and flow. Also, the order in which various parts appear varies from one tradition to another. Furthermore, what is an essential element for one religious tradition may not exist in the basic service of another tradition. By giving a combined presentation of the Protestant, Roman Catholic, and Jewish marriage services, I have put them in a structure that is artificial and does not represent what is the actual structure of any of the rites.

Consequently, the first chapters of this book attempt to define and give examples of the parts of the service. The rest of the book shows how wed-

ding services look from beginning to end, with each part of the service clearly marked.

I invite you to use the book freely to design a service that reflects your values, beliefs and tastes. May you have the wedding that best fits your beliefs and your relationship. Also, may you receive the support of your clergy, family and friends as you plan the wedding that is right for you.

I hope you will take the promises and commitments you make on your wedding day very seriously. However, I also hope you will relax and have fun as you sanctify your new life together. Remember, the touch of your hands, the hugs you exchange, the smiles of joy in your eyes as you and your partner exchange glances, are as important as the ritual and the words. So lighten up. Enjoy the celebration of the relationship. Laugh. A sense of humor is a key tool for survival in weddings, marriage and life.

Chapter 1

Where to Begin

Who will officiate at your service? If you are an active member of a church or a temple, you may already know the person you want to officiate at your wedding. If you are not a member of a religious group, your parents may be active in a church or a temple. They may recommend someone to you. You may not be active in a church or a temple but you may have a denomination in which both of you feel comfortable. If this is the case, look in a local phone book for that denomination and call to see who can officiate at the ceremony. You may have a particular religious building in which you want to get married. Ask what rules the owners of the building have about clergy. Some may have a policy that the only clergy who can officiate at a wedding in their building are the clergy who serve that congregation. Others may welcome guest ministers, rabbis or priests.

Remember that the first responsibility of any cleric is to his or her own congregation. If you are not a member of any religious organization, you may need to make several calls. It may take numerous conversations before you find a cleric who is available and with whom you feel comfortable. Clergy with smaller congregations tend to be more willing and able to officiate at weddings. They can take time to work with you in planning the service because they have fewer demands placed on them by their congregations. Also, fees from weddings help supplement their income.

Laws vary from state to state regarding whom a state legally authorizes to officiate at weddings. When you get your marriage license, ask the clerk what the local laws are. Avoid persons who have mail order ordination certificates. Your wedding may not be considered legal. Play it safe. Use a cleric from an established denomination who meets the laws of the state in which you live.

There are many different styles of religious leadership. Try to find someone with whom you are comfortable. Here is an example of an opening phone call:

My name is _____. I am not a member of your church (or your synagogue), but I am looking for a minister (or priest or rabbi) to officiate at my wedding. Do you do weddings for nonmembers?

The date and time of my wedding are _____. Are you available then?

We would like to have our wedding in your church. Is your building available on that date?

Or:

We plan to have the wedding at _____. Would you be willing to officiate at the ceremony at that site?

Do you have a standard service that you always use, or can my fiancé (or fiancée) and I participate in the planning of the ceremony? If you have a standard service, can we see it before the service?

There are several reasons some clerics use a standard service and do not allow the couple to participate in planning or writing the service. First, their religious group may require that everyone use the same service for theological reasons. Second, the cleric you are talking to may be too busy to take the time to plan a different service for each couple.

Third, the cleric may have memorized one service that he or she does repeatedly. This can be effective. People always like a cleric who can deliver a service from memory. It can greatly improve the eye contact. One study showed that people decide if they like a speaker based first on the facial expression of the speaker. Second in importance is the tone of the speaker's voice. Third in importance is the content of the words the speaker says. In other words, when people say they liked the wedding service, in part they are reacting to the facial expression and the sound of the voice of the cleric. Did he or she smile and look at the congregation? Did he or she have a strong, clear voice? A service said from memory can result in good eye contact and a good delivery. However, it also means the couple may not participate fully in the writing of the ceremony.

How much is your honorarium?

A cleric should give you a direct answer to this question. However, because of tradition and because some clergy are uncomfortable talking about money, you may not get a direct answer. In this case I suggest giving the cleric a check of $150 to $500. The size of the fee depends on the size of the wedding and how often you meet with the cleric. It also depends on how far the wedding is from the cleric's office and whether you expect the cleric to attend the rehearsal. If a couple has little money, some clergy will officiate at a simple ceremony in their office free of charge. On the other hand, remember the clergy's presence and participation makes your wedding a legal event. He or she is important to your ceremony. Try to be fair when you offer the honorarium. If you fly in the family priest, minister or rabbi from his or her home in another state, you are responsible for all expenses. He or she will need to check the legal issues regarding officiating at a wedding in your state.

What are your rules regarding photographs during the service?

You may plan to have the wedding videotaped from three different angles. The cleric you are interviewing may refuse to allow photos of any kind during the ceremony. It is better to find this out sooner than later.

How much does it cost to rent your church?

Would you be willing to meet with us _____ (number of) times?

Do you offer or require any type of premarital counseling?

Some clergy offer no premarital counseling. Other clergy offer one hour or more. Some require this counseling. For others it is an option. Politely explore what the qualifications are for this person to provide counseling. Although there are clergy who have a natural talent for counseling, most of us need years of special training before we can do effective work in counseling. If you or your partner feels a need for premarital counseling, trust that feeling and seek out someone with certification. Consider organizations such as the American Association of Marriage and Family Therapists or the American Association of Pastoral Counselors.

You may feel your relationship is healthy but you would like to deepen it. You might wish to take advantage of the "Couples Enrichment" or "Marriage Encounter" programs offered by several religious groups.

These programs began with the ideas of a Catholic priest in Spain, and they have become popular in the United States.

You may meet with a cleric who uses a questionnaire that tries to evaluate your marriage compatibility. For example, David Olson, a psychologist at the University of Minnesota, and his colleagues have devised a 125-item questionnaire they say is 80 percent correct in predicting compatible unions. Over ten years Olson has studied about 400 couples. In association with the questionnaire, he has produced a ten-step counseling program, titled "Prepare," devised to help couples learn to handle disagreements. Olson and his associates say they have trained 20,000 clergy to use this program.

My religious background is _____ and my fiancé's (or fiancée's) religious background is _____. How do you feel about this?

Try to determine whether the cleric and you have the same perspective. The cleric should be honest and direct with you. If you ask a cleric to do something he or she does not feel comfortable with, you need to know. When there are many differences in what you are asking for and what the cleric is willing to provide, it may be best to look elsewhere. Remember, there are many different types of clergy. Find one with whom you can work.

If the answers you receive to these questions satisfy you, set up an appointment to talk in person with the minister, rabbi or priest. Avoid drugs or alcohol when you meet with the cleric and before the service on the day of your wedding. Clergy who have evidence that one or both people getting married are intoxicated may refuse to officiate at the ceremony. If it is difficult for you to imagine going through the appointment with the cleric or going through the wedding without first having a drink or two, hold off on the wedding. Look at your use of drugs and alcohol.

If you are not a member of the congregation of the cleric performing the ceremony, don't be surprised if you are asked by the cleric to pay in advance or pay a deposit. People sometimes reserve a cleric and a religious building and then decide not to get married, move the wedding to another site or elope and do not notify the cleric they had previously reserved. An advance deposit helps deal with this problem.

If you pay the day of the wedding, give the cleric the marriage license and the check before the service. You will be too busy after the wedding to bother with these details.

What About a Civil Service with a Judge or Justice of the Peace?

Laws vary from state to state, but often a judge or justice of the peace may legally officiate at weddings. In Chicago I called the Cook County Clerk's office. The person who answered told me that judges could legally officiate at weddings, but not justices of the peace. She gave me the court phone number that she provides to couples looking for a judge. I called. After explaining that I was writing a book on wedding services, I asked if there was a civil service that judges use that I could include in the book. "Every judge uses his or her own service. They are all different. The only thing they have in common is that they are all short. The services last about three minutes." Could you send me an example of a ceremony that a judge uses? "No. They are all different. Try the library." Could I speak to a judge? "No. The judges are all busy." Could you take a message and ask a judge to call me? "Well, I will take your name and number, but I doubt that they will return your call. The Cook County court system is the biggest, busiest court system in the world." I tried one more time. Is there anyone else to whom you refer couples, besides the judges at the court? "Where do you live?" After I told her, she said, "Here is the name and phone number of a retired judge who does weddings."

I called the retired judge. His secretary took a message, and he called me back within an hour. He was cordial. We had a short, but delightful conversation. "Since I retired five years ago, I have officiated at one thousand weddings." What text do you use? "I have no service. Each couple puts together their own service. They write it out and give it to me to read. I don't add anything. We go into the service with both the couple and I knowing exactly what I am going to say. The quality of the service varies greatly from couple to couple. I officiated at a remarkable wedding this past weekend. The groom is a professional actor. The wedding was theatrical. It was a Jewish-Christian interfaith service. Many services I do are interfaith."

In an hour I had found a friendly retired judge who gives couples freedom to select or write their own wedding services. Every community is different. It might be easier or harder to find such a person in your community.

If you are uncomfortable with clergy, call the local government office that issues marriage licenses and start asking questions. Be polite and persistent.

The appendices of this book do include an example of a civil ceremony. It is used in New York City's city hall weddings. Short and to the point, it may be the right service for persons who are shy or persons who prefer a modest ritual.

The Basic Parts

of a

Traditional Wedding Ceremony

Chapter 2

The Opening Words

"Why Do You Want to Get Married?"

A groom and bride were sitting in my office. We had never met before. It was their first visit with me to plan their wedding ceremony. "It helps me in preparing for a wedding service to ask a few questions just to get to know you a little better. Why do you want to get married?"

"Because we love each other," said the bride.

"What does the word love mean to you?"

"You know. We love each other. When we are together, we have fun. We want to be together always." She was looking directly at me. "You know the word love is difficult to define."

She was right, of course. Nevertheless, at the beginning of most weddings clergy give a brief statement about why we have gathered. These are general statements, short sermons. Often these statements attempt to define love and marriage and give a theological rationale for both. The question a couple should ask is, "Are we comfortable with this statement about love? Does it describe our relationship?"

How you feel about the word love will depend on several factors. Books on birth order propose the theory that when we marry we try to recreate the family experiences we had as children. For example you may be a second-born male, with an older sister born four years before you. You may find yourself marrying a woman who is a firstborn, four years older than you, with younger brothers. The theory is that we tend to replicate the familiar. When we say, "We're in love," what we are saying is, "This relationship feels splendid and amazing because it is like something with which I already have a great deal of experience."

According to this theory, the couple most in love is the couple who can come closest to repeating the patterns of their childhood. For example, you may be a twenty-two-year-old woman who grew up in a family with an older brother who is now twenty-six. You might fall deeply in love with a man who is twenty-six and has a sister age twenty-two. You might say, "We were meant for each other," without knowing why you feel this. On the other hand, according to the theory, middle children are less likely to feel as passionate about their mate. Consider, for example, a woman with an older brother and a younger brother. She loves her partner, who is the same age as her older brother. However, she may be aware at some level that he is not the only person she could have married. The wedding service they write may have fewer passionate statements about their love for each other.

Another underlying factor that may influence the words in your wedding service is your ethnic background. Books such as *Ethnicity and Family Therapy*, edited by Monica McGoldrick, John K. Pearce and Joseph Giordano, explore these cultural differences. For example, German-Americans tend to define the word love as what people do, not what people say. When it comes to love, German-Americans tend to feel that actions speak louder than words. They might say: "You know I love you not because I say 'I love you' ten times a day but because of what I do. Everyday I rub your back. Once a week I fix you a special meal. When I do the household tasks, I let you sleep in. I earn a steady income that I share with you. I don't drink or get sexually involved with others. By these actions, I show that I love you, which is far more important than any words." The German-American writer Kurt Vonnegut, Jr., writes "To hell with love, and hooray for something else, which I can't even begin to name or describe."

In contrast, if you come from an Italian-American family, you may be comfortable with dramatic, powerful, intense, verbal expressions of love during your wedding service. The words in an Italian-American wedding may be more colorful and express more emotion and feeling. If this is your cultural background, you may find yourself looking for a wedding reading in the writings of someone like Leo Buscaglia.

Sometimes when people talk about the "Perfect Wedding" what they are really talking about is a wedding that best reflects the ethnic and personal values of their childhood. Our birth order in our family of origin plays

a role in what we mean by the word love. Our ethnic heritage influences what we mean by love. And many other factors also influence our definition of love. In some ways, what we mean by love will always be a mystery.

The opening words in this chapter represent the attempt by a few persons to speak about this mystery. More traditional words in the Christian and Jewish services include references to God. The contemporary examples include some examples of opening words that refer to God and some that do not. Read them and see which ones speak to you.

Protestant Ceremony

In these opening words the celebrant says the full names of the persons getting married. Subsequently in the service the cleric uses only the couple's first names.

Dearly beloved: We have come together in the presence of God to witness and bless the joining together of this man and this woman in Holy Matrimony. The bond and covenant of marriage was established by God in creation, and our Lord Jesus Christ adorned this manner of life by his presence and first miracle at a wedding in Cana of Galilee. It signifies to us the mystery of the union between Christ and his Church, and Holy Scripture commends it to be honored among all people. The union of husband and wife in heart, body and mind is intended by God for their mutual joy; for the help and comfort given one another in property and adversity; and, when it is God's will, for the procreation of children and their nurture in the knowledge and love of the Lord. Therefore marriage is not to be entered into unadvisedly or lightly; but reverently, deliberately, and in accordance with the purposes for which it was instituted by God.

Into this holy union _____ and _____ now come to be joined. If any of you can show just cause why they may not lawfully be married, speak now; or else forever hold your peace.

Then the celebrant says to the persons to be married:

I require and charge you both here in the presence of God, that if either of you know any reason why you may not be united in marriage lawfully, and in accordance with God's Word, you do now confess it.

Book of Common Prayer

Roman Catholic Ceremony

The Catholic marriage rite begins with a greeting. At the door of the church or, if more suitable, at the altar, the priest gives the bride and groom a friendly welcome. He shows that the church shares their joy. The priest follows this greeting with an opening prayer or exhortation. The rite gives four different prayers from which to choose. Normally the couple will choose which one they want the priest to use. One of the four prayers follows.

Father, you have made the bond of marriage a holy mystery, a symbol of Christ's Love for his church. Hear our prayers for _____ and _____. With faith in you and in each other they pledge their love today. May their lives always bear witness to the reality of that love. We ask you this through our Lord Jesus Christ, your Son, Who lives and reigns with you and the Holy Spirit, one God, forever and ever.

Rite of Marriage

Jewish Ceremony

Words in parentheses are optional.

Our God at this sacred moment (in the quiet of your house) we pray for Your blessings upon these Your Children. They come into Your presence with precious gifts: (their youth), their love, their hopes and dreams, their faith in each other, and their trust in You. As they consecrate these gifts to Your service, we pray that they may find life's deep-

est meaning and richest happiness. Bind their lives together, O God, in sanctity and in devotion. Teach them to ennoble life as they share their love together. Blessed are you who come here in the name of God. (We bless you in this House of God.) Serve God with Gladness; come before God with singing. O God supremely blessed, supreme in might and glory, guide and bless this bridegroom and this bride.

Rabbi's Manual

Contemporary Ceremony

Friends, _____ and _____ have invited us here today to share in the celebration of their marriage—their wedding.

We come together not to mark the start of a relationship, but to recognize a bond that already exists. This marriage is one expression of the many varieties of love. Love is one, though its expressions are infinite.

It is fitting to speak briefly about love. We live in a world of joy and fear and search for meaning and strength in the seeming disorder. We discover the truest guideline to our quest when we realize love in all its magnitudes. Love is the eternal force of life. Love is the force that allows us to face fear and uncertainty with courage.

But, you must "be of love a little more careful than of anything."

For the giving of yourself in love is difficult, for you must learn to give of your love without total submission of yourself. Therefore, in your giving, give your joy, your sadness, your interest, your understanding, your knowledge—all expressions that make up life. But in this giving, remember to preserve yourself—your integrity, your individuality. This is the challenge of love within marriage.   Source Unknown

• • •

_____ and _____, you are marrying because you enjoy each other's company and because you want to be together. You are

marrying because each of you can grow in humanity and in love more fully while touching the other. You are marrying because you can be more trusting of life as lifemates. Keep this understanding of your marriage fresh and alive in the days ahead.

In marriage a family comes into being. Be joyful in your family. Bring to your family an appreciation of the beauty of each other. Bring to your family a sense of comfort and strength. Bring to your family a joy and thankfulness for being together.

Marriage is a good estate. Bring to it joy. Bring to it the joy of this hour. Bring to it the enjoyment of each other.   Rudolph W. Nemser

• • •

Family and friends of _____ and _____, we have gathered to witness the promises that this couple have come to make to each other. We join in prayer for their happiness as a married couple.

Marriage is an intention of God for the human family. When God created us, we were made in the divine image, male and female. God created us to marry and conceive children, to live together as families and to learn how to love one another. This wedding of man and woman is a partnership in caring for each other and for children. Mutuality and independence learned in the family are a great strength of human society. From generation to generation we pass on happy family life. It is a great heritage to inherit.

Although married life is not for everyone, it has provided an opportunity for caring and responsible sexual intimacy that can convey love and create new life. Marital union can mediate spiritual unity in a bodily mode that transcends the limitations of speech. In day-to-day experience a husband and wife can know the meeting of minds, the communion of spirits and the joining of bodies.   David Hostetter

• • •

You have come here today from your varied life experiences to make public the commitment you have made, each to the other. You come to combine your two separate lives into one.

Although you will be sharing one life, never forget, you are two separate people. Cherish and affirm your differences. Love each other. Keep your commitment primary. Together you will laugh and cry, be sick and well, be happy and angry, share and grow.

Grow, sometimes together, sometimes separately. But never remain stagnant. Love and life are always changing, always new.

If you will ensure a healthy lasting marriage, always, always value each other. Although you will disagree, remember to respect each other's feelings, needs and wants. And above all, never, never lose your sense of humor.   Joan Kahn-Schneider

• • •

> Love is a gift
>> from out of the stars and into your hearts:
>> from each of you to the other:
>> from who you are and who you become to the
>>> wider circle of family and friends
>>> who are your community;
>> from each child and parent and caring friend
>> to you, _____, _____;
> Love is a gift, a magnificent mystery.
>
> Love is a hard-earned treasure
>> wrenched from the depths of mortal self-centeredness;
>> at risk in every open and unspoken conflict;
>> part of the struggle to give to the other without
>>> giving yourself away;
>> endlessly demanding of you both repentance
>>> and forgiveness;

every day asking something of you to prove you
are worthy of the grace of such a caring relationship;
Love is a hard-earned treasure, a genuine moral achievement.

Love is a joy
making your eyes light up
and sometimes fill up;
giving you laughter to uplift your souls;
bringing you intense pleasure
at the sound of your beloved's voice
at the very touch of a hand
or lips sweetly embracing;
lifting you from despair and loneliness
to companionship and meaningfulness;
Love is a joy, the richest blessing you can know.

Love is a communion
of your unity with each other;
of your relation to those who are part of
your circle of caring,
children and relatives and friends;
of your feelings for each other
focused in this special moment but enduring
through the past,
in the present,
and into the future;
of our feelings for you
as we have known you,
as we know you now,
as we will know you in the days ahead;
of your ties to the earth,
to air and water and fire,
to worms and winged creatures and wolverine,
to woman and man,
to life itself;

Love is a communion, the circle within which we all
live and move and have our being.

_____ and _____:
May all that you are always be in love;
May all that is love always be in you.
May your love be as beautiful on each day you share
    as it is on this day of celebration.

                                        Kenneth W. Phifer

• • •

My friends, we have gathered today in the midst of verdant spring, a
time for new beginnings in relationships, as well as in nature. Yet while
the first flowers of spring are gorgeous to behold, compellingly sweet to
the senses, we know that it takes several seasons, much tender care and
the weathering of many storms for the fruit of those perennial flowers
to grow and ripen. Similarly, it takes time for love to mature and reach
its rightful completion.

This spring wedding ought to remind us that, like the seasons, human
life—the life of the spirit and the emotions—moves in cycles. To be in a
loving relationship does not guarantee an eternal summer. To make a
sincere and honest commitment does not promise an end to all struggle.
What a good relationship does offer is opportunity for renewal. It recog-
nizes the abiding, shared hope that after every winter, spring will come
again.

In marriage we make a commitment to weather patiently the cold and
bitter times, to protect and tend that original love-seed until it bursts
into bloom again.

We are here to celebrate beginnings, and to acknowledge that love, as
anything else we would have abide for long, requires sustaining care
and nurture. In making this declaration to their family and friends,

_____ and _____ express their eagerness to take up this lifelong challenge in seriousness and in joy.   Michael A. Schuler

• • •

Dear friends, on this warm and friendly May afternoon, our fondness for two special people draws us here, that we might bear witness to the light that illumines their lives.

My friends, I would suggest that a good relationship must contain two features—the practical and the transcendent. They must be so integrated that one does not suffer neglect at the expense of the other.

In this age of self-help books and support groups, a good deal is said about the pragmatic marriage. We are reminded constantly of the importance of communication skills, mutual consideration, providing a space for each party to grow and fulfill him or herself. And we are told that love alone won't sustain a relationship, that we shouldn't be led out on a limb by the romantic impulse.

All of this is good advice, yet it ought not lead us to the opposite conclusion—that love isn't as crucial for the success of a marriage as a no-loophole prenuptial agreement.

On the contrary, love is essential, and when I speak of love I mean that feeling we all hope to have that there is someone else in the world whose welfare we are as committed to as our own. And this is what I mean by the "transcendent" aspect of marriage. It is the readiness to come out of ourselves, radically to extend ourselves, for the sake of another. To find this kind of love is, as the poet Evelyn Barkins said, "Beyond the bounds of logic and common sense, it is the gift sublime." And from what I have observed of _____ and _____, I think their relationship exhibits something of this selfless, spiritual quality.

Sometimes the chemistry of love works explosively, like dynamite; other times it works gradually, more like oxidation. It really depends on the temperament of the individuals and the circumstances of their romance. But it doesn't matter how or when it happens, so long as that miraculous sensation, that authentic ardor, is really present.

This conviction of love makes all the difference in the world, because otherwise we are merely going through the motions of marriage. Granted, love alone is not enough to make a relationship work; but without it all the practical advice in the world is powerless to make our lives any richer, or deeper, or more generous.   Michael A. Schuler

• • •

_____ and _____, in presenting yourselves here today to be joined in holy union, you perform an act of faith. This faith can grow and mature and endure, but only if you both determine to make it so. A lasting and growing love is never automatic, nor guaranteed by any ceremony.

If you would have the foundation of your union be the love you have for each other, not just at this moment, but for all the days ahead, then cherish the hopes and dreams that you bring here today. Resolve that your love will never be blotted out by the commonplace nor obscured by the ordinary in life. Faults will appear where now you find content-ment, and wonder can be crushed by the routine of daily living.

Devotion, joy and love can grow only if you nurture them together. Stand fast in that hope and confidence, believing in your shared future just as strongly as you believe in yourselves and in each other today. Only in this spirit, can you create a partnership that will strengthen and sustain you all the days of your lives.   Angeline E. M. Theisen

• • •

We have come together today in the presence of God to witness the joining of _____ and _____ in Holy Matrimony. This is a special time of celebration that _____ and _____ will long remember, and because of this, they are thankful you are here to share their joy. From the dawn of human history, it has been customary for the community to place its seal of approval upon the union of two persons in marriage. If these solemn vows that they are about to make are kept faithfully, God will bless their marriage.

Gracious God, before whom we stand: Look with favor upon this man and this woman who desire to make their vows before you and this gathering of family and friends. We are grateful for their families, which have reared them to maturity; and for the church, which has nurtured them in the faith. May they experience your presence as they pledge their lives, one to another, and may they ever walk the pleasant paths of righteousness. This we pray through Christ our Lord. Amen.

Richard W. Thomas

Chapter 3

The Readings

"Stand Together, Yet Not Too Near Together"

"Do you have any favorite readings that you would like to use as part of the service?" I asked the couple.

There was a pause. "No. I hadn't thought of any," said the groom. He looked at the bride, and she shook her head.

"What do other people normally have?" she asked me. In response, I showed her the following four readings that are used most often in weddings.

The New Testament

Paul wrote First Corinthians, chapter 13, as a letter to a small Christian group about twenty or twenty-five years after the death of Jesus. After A.D. 50 the new religion of Christianity was spreading rapidly across the Mediterranean area. There were many new, growing groups, and there were many political restrictions placed on Paul's travels. Therefore, he began to keep in contact with the new groups, writing letters in Greek on large sheets of papyrus. He sent out personal letters to each congregation, intended to be read to the group when they gathered to share in a ritual meal. In these letters he tried to respond to questions about proper conduct. Because informa-

21

tion was so meager in those early years of the Christian church, Christians often copied these letters and sent them around to other nearby churches.

Paul was preparing people for the second coming of Jesus, whom he believed was the Messiah. Today most Biblical scholars believe that Paul thought this second coming was only a few years away, perhaps only a few months away. Paul's letters, intended to guide these small churches for a short time until Jesus returned, are today two thousand-year-old scriptures.

There are many different translations. One commonly used in weddings is the English translation completed in 1611, which today is called the Authorized Version (AV) in England and the King James Version (KJV) in America. When using this translation today, most people replace the word "charity" with the word "love." This translation is likely to be familiar to many persons who have attended wedding services. Many of them may have used it at their own service. They may have heard it at other weddings or as a reading in church. For many people it is still *the* Bible, with its phrases and images deeply embedded in English-speaking cultural history. When you use this reading, you may elicit in people the positive associations they have with these words. These positive associations come from hearing these words in the past during meaningful times in their lives.

There are many other English translations. The New Revised Standard Version, first published in 1989, is gaining wide acceptance among mainline Protestants. Scholars consider the NRSV the most accurate revision of the King James Version. Many Protestants also use the Good News Bible, published in 1976 by the American Bible Society. Roman Catholics use the New American Bible and the Jerusalem Bible. The advantage of using a modern English translation is that it is much more understandable. However, modern translations do not carry the long emotional associations that the traditional King James Version carries.

The translators of the King James Version placed some words in italics to show to the reader that these specific words were not present in the Greek text. The translators inserted the italicized words for clarification. Below is the most often used reading in American wedding services, although most ministers, priests and couples change the word charity to love.

Though I speak with the tongues of men and of angels, and have not charity, I am become *as* sounding brass, or a tinkling cymbal. And

though I have *the gift of* prophecy, and understand all mysteries, and all knowledge; and though I have all faith, so that I could remove mountains, and have not charity, I am nothing. And though I bestow all my goods to feed *the poor*, and though I give my body to be burned, and have not charity, it profiteth me nothing.

Charity suffereth long *and* is kind; charity envieth not; charity vaunteth not itself, is not puffed up; Doth not behave itself unseemly, seeketh not her own, is not easily provoked, thinketh no evil; Rejoiceth not in iniquity, but rejoiceth in the truth; Beareth all things, believeth all things, hopeth all things, endureth all things.

Charity never faileth: but whether *there be* prophecies, they shall fail; whether *there be* tongues, they shall cease; whether *there be* knowledge, it shall vanish away. For we know in part, and we prophesy in part. But when that which is perfect is come, then that which is in part shall be done away. When I was a child, I spake as a child, I understood as a child, I thought as a child: but when I became a man, I put away childish things. For now we see through a glass, darkly; but then face to face: now I know in part; but then shall I know even as also I am known. And now abideth faith, hope, charity, these three, but the greatest of these *is* charity.

1 Cor. 13, Authorized (King James) Version

The New Revised Standard Version, below, has the advantage of the most recent biblical research and uses twentieth century English.

If I speak in the tongues of mortals and of angels, but do not have love, I am a noisy gong or a clanging cymbal. And if I have prophetic powers, and understand all mysteries and all knowledge, and if I have all faith, so as to remove mountains, but do not have love, I am nothing. If I give away all my possessions, and if I hand over my body so that I may boast, but do not have love, I gain nothing.

Love is patient; love is kind; love is not envious or boastful or arrogant or rude. It does not insist on its own way; it is not irritable or resentful; it does not rejoice in wrongdoing, but rejoices in the truth. It bears all things, believes all things, hopes all things, endures all things.

Love never ends. But as for prophecies, they will come to an end; as for tongues, they will cease; as for knowledge, it will come to an end. For we know only in part, and we prophesy only in part; but when the complete comes, the partial will come to an end. When I was a child, I spoke like a child, I thought like a child, I reasoned like a child; when I became an adult, I put an end to childish ways. For now we see in a mirror dimly, but then we will see face to face. Now I know only in part; then I will know fully, even as I have been fully known. And now faith, hope, and love abide, these three; and the greatest of these is love.

1 Cor. 13, New Revised Standard Version

The Old Testament or Hebrew Scriptures

If there were ratings for the books of the Hebrew Scriptures, the Song of Songs (also translated as the Song of Solomon) would be rated "R." Full of elaborate imagery, it is a collection of steamy love poems, with no references to God. There are no other writings remotely like it anywhere else in the Bible. The Song of Songs is popular at weddings because it is full of folk poetry that affirms the beauty of nature and of the human body.

There are many different interpretations of the book. Some believe the groom in the story is symbolic of God and the bride is symbolic of the Jewish nation. For others the story is about two lovers, or two lovers and a king. For still others, this book consists of wedding poems. According to this theory, the poems were part of the seven-day wedding festivities among Syrian peasants. They treated the groom and bride as king and queen. To honor them, the peasants recited poems describing the physical beauty of the couple. Yet another view is that the book is an anthology of secular love poems. According to this belief, they were collected over five hundred years from the tenth century B.C. to the fifth century B.C.

A prevailing interpretation is that the poems in the Song of Songs are from

" . . . ancient Hebrew New Year liturgies that celebrated the reunion and marriage of the sun god with the mother goddess, which in the ancient world typified the revival of life in nature that came with the return of the growing season. It is the literary residue of a myth, a liturgy of life; it harks back to the ancient fertility cult which in its many forms was

24

found throughout the whole world and is not without its survivals even in our own day, as witness features in our Easter celebration."[1]

The passage below is often used in wedding ceremonies.

> The voice of my beloved!
>   Look he comes,
> leaping upon the mountains,
>   bounding over the hills.
> My beloved is like a gazelle
>   or a young stag.
> Look, there he stands
>   behind our wall,
> gazing in at the windows,
>   looking through the lattice.
> My beloved speaks and says to me:
> "arise, my love, my fair one,
>   and come away;
> O my dove, in the clefts of the rock,
>   In the covert of the cliff,
> let me see your face,
>   let me hear your voice;
> for your voice is sweet,
>   and your face is lovely.
> My beloved is mine and I am his;
> Set me as a seal upon your heart,
>   as a seal upon your arm;
> for love is strong as death,
>   passion fierce as the grave.
> Its flashes are flashes of fire,
>   a raging flame.
> Many waters cannot quench love,
>   neither can floods drown it.

> *Song of Songs 2:8–10, 14, 16a; 8:6–7a*
> *New Revised Standard Version*

---

[1]*The Interpreter's Bible*, volume 5, page 94.

Sonnet 116 by William Shakespeare

Many couples want more than one reading at their wedding, or they prefer a reading from a source other than the Bible. This is particularly true of a marriage in which one person in the relationship is from a non-Christian background. A common reading often used in weddings is Sonnet 116 by William Shakespeare.

Shakespeare was born about 1564 and died in 1616; his sonnets were first published in 1609. The sonnets may describe the author's association with various persons, or they may have been written as a story, of which each sonnet is one small part. They express forceful emotions in a restricted word structure.

If you were not an English major in school, you may find Sonnet 116 difficult to grasp. The references in the poem may have been easy to follow in England four hundred years ago, but many are not commonly understood today. Here is a rough translation: Shakespeare is saying that he does not wish to interfere in the marriage of two people who love each other. He then proceeds to define love. He says that love is not true love, if it changes when the couple disagrees, or if it changes when the loved one is not always perfect. Love, says Shakespeare, is as reliable as the North Star is to the mariner during stormy weather, never changing position in the sky. We can depend on love in the same way sailors in their ships (wandering bark) depend on the North Star by which to navigate. The nature of the star (and the nature of love) is unknown, although the navigator can measure the height of the star from the horizon. Love does not change as time passes, although physical beauty (rosy lips and cheeks) dies with time. Love does not change over hours or weeks but stays the same, even to doomsday. Shakespeare ends the sonnet by saying you can never prove him wrong on the subject of love because it is obvious that he wrote many plays and poems, and that many people have loved.

Like scriptural readings, it takes careful practice to read Sonnet 116 well. However, like familiar scriptural readings, it can bring forth strong positive feelings in the guests at a wedding service. If you ask a friend or relative to read this at a wedding, encourage them to practice it aloud several times before the service.

Let me not to the marriage of true minds
Admit impediments. Love is not love
Which alters when it alteration finds
Or bends with the remover to remove.
O, no, it is an ever fixed mark
That looks on tempests and is never shaken,
It is the star to every wandering bark,
Whose worth's unknown, although his height be taken.
Love's not time's fool, though rosy lips and cheeks
Within his bending sickle's compass come,
Love alters not with his brief hours and weeks,
But bears it out even to the edge of doom:
  If this be error, and upon me proved,
  I never writ, nor no man ever loved.

Sonnet 116,
William Shakespeare

A Passage by Kahlil Gibran

Many people have not studied Shakespeare's Sonnet 116, and their reaction to hearing it read at your wedding will be "I don't know what this poem means." Some couples may prefer a reading written in modern English that all the people who come to the wedding service can understand. There is a fourth reading commonly used in weddings. It is from *The Prophet*, written by the romantic essayist Kahlil Gibran and published in 1923. Born in 1883 in Lebanon, Gibran immigrated with his parents to Boston in 1895. In 1912 he settled in New York City and devoted himself to writing and painting.

In this passage from *The Prophet* Gibran says that partners who are getting married should not lose their individuality after their marriage. Because this desire not to lose our individual identity is strong in British-American culture, the passage is often read in weddings.

Love one another, but make not a bond of love:
Let it rather be a moving sea between the shores of your
souls.

Fill each other's cup but drink not from one cup.
Give one another of your bread but eat not from the same
loaf.
Sing and dance together and be joyous, but let each one of
you be alone,
Even as the strings of a lute are alone though they quiver
with the same music.

Give your hearts, but not into each other's keeping.
For only the hand of Life can contain your hearts.
And stand together yet not too near together:
For the pillars of the temple stand apart,
And the oak tree and the cypress grow not in each other's
shadow.

The Prophet,
Kahlil Gibran

Additional Readings

The readings that follow are also used in wedding services. In selecting
a reading, trust your feelings. What words describe your feeling for your
partner and your understanding of your relationship?

Here in the space between us and the world
lies human meaning.

Into the vast uncertainty we call.

The echoes make our music,
sharp equations which can hold the stars,
and marvelous mythologies we trust.

This may be all we need
to lift our love against indifference and pain.

Here in the space between us and each other
lies all the future
of the fragment of the universe
which is our own.

From *Sound of Silence,*
Raymond J. Baughan

. . .

The meaning of marriage begins in the giving of words. We cannot join ourselves to one another without giving our word. And this must be an unconditional giving, for in joining ourselves to one another we join ourselves to the unknown. We can join one another only by joining the unknown. We must not be misled by the procedures of experimental thought: in life, in the world, we are never given two known results to choose between, but only one result that we choose without knowing what it is.

Marriage rests upon the immutable *givens* that compose it: words, bodies, characters, histories, places. Some wishes cannot succeed; some victories cannot be won; some loneliness is incorrigible. But there is relief and freedom in knowing what is real; these givens come to us out of the perennial reality of the world, like the terrain we live on. One does not care for this ground to make it a different place, or to make it perfect, but to make it inhabitable and to make it better. To flee from its realities is only to arrive at them unprepared.

Because the condition of marriage is worldly and its meaning communal, no one party to it can be solely in charge. What you alone think it ought to be, it is not going to be. Where you alone think you want it to go, it is not going to go. It is going where the two of you—and marriage, time, life, history, and the world—will take it. You do not know the road; you have committed your life to a way.

From *Standing by Words,*
Wendell Berry

. . .

How do I love thee? Let me count the ways.
I love thee to the depth and breadth and height
My soul can reach, when feeling out of sight
For the ends of Being and ideal Grace.
I love thee to the level of everyday's
Most quiet need, by sun and candle-light.
I love thee freely, as men strive for Right;
I love thee purely, as they turn from Praise.
I love thee with the passion put to use
In my old griefs, and with my childhood's faith.
I love thee with a love I seemed to lose
With my lost saints,—I love thee with the breath,
Smiles, tears, of all my life!—and, if God choose,
I shall love thee better after death.

Elizabeth Barrett Browning

•   •   •

If thou must love me, let it be for naught
Except for love's sake only. Do not say
"I love her for her smile—her look—her way
Of speaking gently,—for a trick of thought
That falls in well with mine, and certes brought
A sense of pleasant ease on such a day"—
For these things in themselves, Beloved, may
Be changed, or change for thee—and love, so wrought,
May be unwrought so. Neither love me for
Thine own dear pity's wiping my cheeks dry:
A creature might forget to weep, who bore
Thy comfort long, and love thy love thereby!
But love me for love's sake, that evermore
Thou mayst love on, through love's eternity.

Elizabeth Barrett Browning

•   •   •

i like my body when it is with your
body. It is so quite new a thing.
Muscles better and nerves more.
i like your body. i like what it does,
i like its hows. i like to feel the spine
of your body and its bones, and the trembling
-firm-smooth ness and which i will
again and again and again
kiss, i like kissing this and that of you,
i like, slowly stroking the, shocking fuzz
of your electric fur, and what-is-it comes
over parting flesh . . . . And eyes big love-crumbs,

and possibly i like the thrill

of under me you so quite new

e.e. cummings

• • •

Love is the simplest of all earthly things.
It needs no grandeur of celestial trust
In more than what it is, no holy wings:
It stands with honest feet in honest dust.
And is the body's blossoming in clear air
Of trustfulness and joyance when alone
Two mortals pass beyond the hour's despair
And claim that Paradise which is their own.
Amid a universe of sweat and blood,
Beyond the glooms of all the nations' hate,
Lovers, forgetful of the poisoned mood
Of the loud world, in secret ere too late
A gentle sacrament may celebrate
Before their private altar of the good.

Arthur Davison Ficke

• • •

For everything there is a season, and a time for every
matter under heaven:
a time to be born, and a time to die
a time to plant, and a time to pluck up what is planted;
a time to kill, and a time to heal;
a time to break down, and a time to build up,
a time to weep, and a time to laugh;
a time to mourn, and a time to dance;
a time to throw away stones, and a time to gather stones
together;
a time to embrace, and a time to refrain from embracing;
a time to seek, and a time to lose;
a time to keep, and a time to throw away;
a time to tear, and a time to sew;
a time to keep silence, and a time to speak;
a time for love, and a time for hate;
a time for war, and a time for peace.

Ecclesiastes 3:1-8,
New Revised Standard Version

Following the *Ecclesiastes* reading the officiant might say: "For everything
there is a season, and a time for every matter under heaven. Now is a time
for a wedding."

. . .

What greater thing is there for two human souls than to feel that they
are joined for life, to strengthen each other in all labor, to rest on each
other in all sorrow, to minister to each other in all pain, to be one with
each other in silent unspeakable memories at the moment of the last
parting?

From *Adam Bede,*
George Eliot

. . .

32

Can one have love? If we could, love would need to be a thing, a substance that one can have, own, possess. The truth is, there is no such thing as "love." "Love" is abstraction, perhaps a goddess or an alien being, although nobody has ever seen this goddess. In reality, there exists only the act of loving. To love is a productive activity. It implies caring for, knowing, responding, affirming, enjoying: the person, the tree, the painting, the idea. It means bringing to life, increasing his/her/its aliveness. It is a process, self-renewing and self-increasing . . .

To say "I have a great love for you," is meaningless. Love is not a thing that one can have, but a *process*, an inner activity that one is the subject of. I can love, I can *be* in love, but in loving, I *have* . . . nothing. In fact, the less I have the more I can love.

From *To Have or to Be?*,
Erich Fromm

• • •

Marriage has certain qualities of contract, in which two people take on the housekeeping tasks of living, together, to enhance life's joy.

However, marriage is more than a contract. Marriage is commitment to take that joy deep, deeper than happiness, deep into the discovery of who you most truly are. It is a commitment to a spiritual journey, to a life of becoming—in which joy can comprehend despair, running through rivers of pain into joy again.

And thus marriage is even deeper than commitment. It is a covenant—a covenant that says:

> I love you.
> I trust you.
> I will be here for you when you are hurting,
> and when I am hurting, I will not leave.

It is a covenant intended not to provide haven from pain or from anger and sorrow. Life offers no such haven. Instead, marriage is intended to provide a sanctuary safe enough to risk loving, to risk living and sharing from the center of oneself. This is worth everything.

Margaret A. Keip

• • •

The hand which you each offer
to the other
is an extension of yourselves;
just as is the warmth and love
which you express to each other.
Cherish the touch,
for you are touching another life.
Be sensitive to its pulse,
and try to understand and respect its flow and rhythm,
just as you do your own.

Paul L' Herrou

• • •

If your love is to grow and deepen,
you must find a way to move
with each other;

perhaps in a slow and graceful dance
(bare feet firmly feeling the ground),
a dance, that circles and tests
and learns
as it gradually moves closer
to that place
where you can each
pass through the other
and turn and embrace
without breaking
or losing any part of yourselves
but only to learn more of who you each are
by your touching,

to find that you are each whole
and individual and separate
yet, in the same instant,
one, joined as a whole
that does not blur the two individuals
as you dance.

The music is there
if you will listen hard,
through the static and noise of life,
and other tunes that fill your heads.

You are here,
marking time to the music.

The dance can only begin
if you will take the first (and hardest)
tentative,
uncertain,
stumbling
steps.

Paul L'Herrou

• • •

When you love someone you do not love them all the time, in exactly
the same way, from moment to moment. It is an impossibility. It is even
a lie to pretend to. And yet this is exactly what most of us demand. We
have so little faith in the ebb and flow of life, of love, of relationships.
We leap at the flow of the tide and resist in terror its ebb. We are afraid
it will never return. We insist on permanency, on duration, on continuity; when the only continuity possible, in life as in love, is in growth, in
fluidity—in freedom, in the sense that the dancers are free, barely
touching as they pass, but partners in the same pattern.

The only real security is not in owning or possessing, not in demanding
or expecting, not in hoping, even. Security in a relationship lies neither

in looking back to what it was in nostalgia, nor forward to what it might be in dread or anticipation, but living in the present relationship and accepting it as it is now. For relationships, too, must be like islands, one must accept them for what they are here and now, within their limits— islands, surrounded and interrupted by the sea, and continually visited and abandoned by the tides. One must accept the security of the winged life, of the ebb and flow, of intermittency.

From *Gift from the Sea*,
Anne Morrow Lindbergh

• • •

Come live with me and be my love,
And we will all the pleasures prove
That valleys, groves, hills, and fields,
Woods, or steepy mountain yields.
And we will sit upon the rocks,
Seeing the shepherds feed their flocks,
By shallow rivers to whose falls
Melodious birds sing madrigals.

And I will make thee beds of roses
And a thousand fragrant posies,
A cap of flowers, and a kirtle
Embroidered all with leaves of myrtle;

A gown made of the finest wool
Which from our pretty lambs we pull;
Fair lined slippers for the cold,
With buckles of the purest gold;

A belt of straw and ivy buds,
With coral clasps and amber studs:
And if these pleasures may thee move,
Come live with me, and be my love.

The shepherds' swains shall dance and sing
For thy delight each May morning:
If these delights thy mind may move,
Then live with me and be my love.

Christopher Marlowe

. . .

A portion of your soul has been
     entwined with mine.
A gentle kind of togetherness, while
     separate we stand.
As two trees deeply rooted in
     separate plots of ground,
While their topmost branches
     come together,
Forming a miracle of lace
     against the heavens.

"Two Trees,"
Janet Miles

. . .

It takes years to marry completely two hearts, even of the most loving and well assorted. A happy wedlock is a long falling in love. Young persons think love belongs only to the brown-haired and crimson-cheeked. So it does for its beginning. But the golden marriage is a part of love which the Bridal day knows nothing of.

A perfect and complete marriage, where wedlock is everything you could ask and the ideal of marriage becomes actual, is not common, perhaps as rare as perfect personal beauty. Men and women are married fractionally, now a small fraction, then a large fraction. Very few are married totally, and they only after some forty or fifty years of gradual approach and experiment.

Such a large and sweet fruit is a complete marriage that it needs a long summer to ripen in, and then a long winter to mellow and season it. But

a real, happy marriage of love and judgment between a noble man and woman is one of the things so very handsome that if the sun were, as the Greek poets fabled, a God, he might stop the world and hold it still now and then in order to look all day long on some example thereof, and feast his eyes on such a spectacle.

Theodore Parker

. . .

The institution of marriage was begun
  that a man and a woman
    might learn how to love
      and, in loving, know joy;
  that a man and a woman
    might learn how to share pain and loneliness
      and, in sharing, know strength;
  that a man and a woman
    might learn how to give
      and, in giving know communion.

The institution of marriage was begun
  that a man and a woman
    might through their joy,
      their strength, and their communion,
  become creators of life itself.

Marriage is a high and holy state,
  to be held
    in honor
      among all men and women.

Marriage is a low and common state,
  to be built
    of the stuff
      of daily life.

Men and women are not angels, nor are they gods.
    Love can become hatred;
        joy, sorrow,
            marriage, divorce.

But human beings are not condemned to failure.
    Love can grow even in a real world.
        The wounds of sorrow can be healed,
            And new life built on the learnings of the old.

This is the reason for our gathering today:
    to renew our faith
        in the strength of hope
            and the power of love.

                            Kenneth W. Phifer

• • •

You ask what is this love we here affirm, and I answer, it is a covenant you make, one with the other, a covenant born of commitment to each other's well being and growth and commitment to your relationship itself, allowing it the possibility of change and of growth. And so the covenant reads:

Take time for each other and act always from a caring position. Allow each other time alone for renewal and creativity. Be as honest as possible about feelings as well as actions. Share household and routine tasks with role reversal as a reality. Listen to each other with intent beyond the words. Allow other relationships and commitments in your lives. And make room in your covenant for the children of your love and when the time comes to let them go, do so with joy and caring; then come to your primary relationship with fresh commitments to new beginnings.

                            Betty Pingel

• • •

There is an art to marriage as there is to any creative activity we human beings engage in. This art asks that we pay attention to the little things as well as the big ones that are part of the closeness of marriage. Never grow too old to hold hands. At least once each day, remember to say, "I love you." In so much as it is possible, develop the capacity to forgive and forget and heal quarrels as they happen so that you do not go to bed angry. Your courtship should not end with the honeymoon; so pay attention that you do not come to take each other for granted, and remember to speak words of appreciation and demonstrate your gratitude in thoughtful ways.

It is important to have a mutual sense of values and common objectives so that you stand together as you work through the world and do things for each other, not as a duty or sacrifice, but in the spirit of joy. Do not expect perfection of each other; perfection is only for the gods. But do give each other room to grow and cultivate flexibility, patience, understanding, and sense of humor in your relationship. And your marriage is not just for two people. Use it to form a circle of love that gathers in your families and the children who may be part of your lives.

Find room for the things of the spirit and make your search for the good and the beautiful a common search. In the words of a counselor, make yours a relationship in which "the independence is equal, the dependence is mutual, and the obligation is reciprocal." Remember that standing together never means dissolving your individual selves into each other, but indeed means the strengthening of the individuality of each. A good marriage evolves when two distinct souls face life's joy and its sorrow in harmony, not in unison.

This list sounds very long and very heavy, yet it is only a small part of what is required of two people who would truly accept that making a marriage over the years is an artistic endeavor worthy of our best efforts. It is not just another relationship in our lives; it is the one that gives us courage and the support to reach out to other people in love and wholeness.

Betty Pingel

• • •

. . . once the realization is accepted that even between the *closest* human beings infinite distances continue to exist, a wonderful living side by side can grow up, if they succeed in loving the distance between them which makes it possible for each to see the other whole against a wide sky!

From *Letters to a Young Poet,*
Rainer Maria Rilke
Translated by J. B. Greene and M.D.H. Norton

• • •

The Fountains mingle with the River
And the Rivers with the Ocean,
The winds of Heaven mix for ever
With a sweet emotion;
Nothing in the world is single;
All things by a law divine
In one spirit meet and mingle.
Why not I with thine?

See the mountains kiss high Heaven
And the waves clasp one another;
No sister-flower would be forgiven
If it disdained its brother,
And the sunlight clasps the earth
And the moonbeams kiss the sea:
What is all this sweet work worth
If thou kiss not me?

"Love's Philosophy,"
Percy Bysshe Shelley

Love is sensing the other as a presence.
>Love is receiving the feelings, thoughts
>intentions of the other into your
>own understanding.

Love is fidelity over the long haul.
>Without fidelity love is a puff of
>wind, a gust of emotion.

Love is talking together about insignificant
>things and significant things
>until a few important things, words,
>people have similar meanings for
>both of you, and you both know that
>this is so.

Love is listening together to the pulse
>of what-it-means-to-be-alive, to be
>human, to glorify that which is sacred
>and enjoy it.

>>>Edited and adapted from Ross Snyder

· · ·

I do not offer the old smooth prizes,
But offer rough new prizes,
These are the days that must happen to you:
You shall not heap up what is called riches,
You shall scatter with lavish hand all that you
earn or achieve.
However sweet the laid-up stores,
However convenient the dwellings,
You shall not remain there.
However sheltered the port,
And however calm the waters,
You shall not anchor there.
However welcome the hospitality that welcomes you
You are permitted to receive it but a little while
Afoot and lighthearted, take to the open road,

Healthy, free, the world before you,
The long brown path before you, leading wherever
you choose.
Say only to one another:
Camerado, I give you my hand!
I give you my love, more precious than money,
I give you myself before preaching or law:
Will you give me yourself?
Will you come travel with me?
Shall we stick by each other as long as we live?

Walt Whitman

Chapter 4

The Question of Intent

"Do You . . ."

The administrative secretary of the church called me over the intercom and said there was a couple who wanted to see me. Setting aside the sermon I was struggling to write, I invited them into my office. They explained that they wanted to get married in a private ceremony without any witnesses. I explained that in the state we were in, the law required there be two witnesses. They asked whether the church secretary and the sexton could fill that function. I admitted they could. "However," I said, "before I do the ceremony I want to explore with you for a few minutes your reasons why you don't want anyone at your service."

With many people, I share a strong degree of shyness and personal reserve. Also, like many people in society, I need independence. I need to feel that I have an identity separate from others. Therefore, I understand couples who come to me wishing to be married in small private services. There are several common reasons. For some, it is the desire to avoid disapproving relatives, such as a parent who is against the marriage. In other situations, the parents approve but one or more of the parents wants to take charge and direct the wedding. They may push their child away by trying to be in control. Sometimes it is a strong feeling of shyness in the bride or the groom or both. Sometimes it is because the bride or the groom or both are divorced or widowed. For this second wedding, they do not feel the need for a large public service. A lack of money is sometimes the reason. (Some clergy will officiate at simple services in churches and ask no fee.)

In the case of the aforementioned couple, they had moved to the community seven years before, living together in the same apartment. To make life simpler, they had told their new friends that they were married. Now they had decided that they wanted to be legally married. They didn't want to explain to their friends that they had not been telling the truth for seven years. I did a simple service in my office, several days later. My rule in such situations is that I ask people to wait at least two weeks before I will officiate at the service. This gives them a chance to change their minds and have a public wedding.

In contrast to these private services, most weddings are public statements of commitment. In the service, the officiant will ask a question to both the bride and groom; symbolically, the officiant is representing the witnesses, and the community. During this part of the service the bride and groom face the minister, not each other. In effect the minister says, "We want to know why you are here. Are you serious about this? Are you willing to make a major commitment to each other? Many of us in the larger society want to know, Is this going to be a healthy relationship? Will the two of you be responsible and do your best to care for each other and any children you have? Will you add to the health and stability of the community?"

As you can see, a wedding is not just a promise you make to each other. Your wedding is also a commitment you make to your friends and relatives and to society. The question is, "What promise would you like to make to your relatives and to the community?" Here are examples of this part of the service.

Protestant Ceremony

The celebrant says to the woman:

           _____, will you have this man to be your husband; to live together in the covenant of marriage? Will you love him, comfort him, honor and keep him, in sickness and in health; and, forsaking all others, be faithful to him as long as you both shall live?

The woman answers:

I will.

The celebrant says to the man:

_____, will you have this woman to be your wife; to live together in the covenant of marriage? Will you love her, comfort her, honor and keep her, in sickness and in health; and, forsaking all others, be faithful to her as long as you both shall live?

The man answers:

I will.

The celebrant then addresses the congregation, saying:

Will all of you witnessing these promises do all in your power to uphold these two persons in their marriage?

People:

We will.

Book of Common Prayer

Roman Catholic Ceremony

All stand, including the bride and groom, and the priest addresses them in these or similar words:

My dear friends, you have come together in this church so that the Lord may seal and strengthen your love in the presence of the Church's minister and this community. Christ abundantly blesses this love. He has already consecrated you in baptism and now he enriches and strengthens you by a special sacrament so that you may assume the duties of marriage in mutual and lasting fidelity. And so, in the presence of the Church, I ask you to state your intentions.

If marriage is celebrated between a Catholic and an unbaptized person, the following formula is used.

My dear friends, you have come together in this church so that the Lord may seal and strengthen your love in the presence of the Church's minister and this community. In this way you will be strengthened to keep mutual and lasting fidelity with each other and to carry out the other duties of marriage. And so, in the presence of the Church, I ask you to state your intentions.

The priest then questions them about their freedom of choice, faithfulness to each other and the acceptance and upbringing of children:

_____ and _____, have you come here freely and without reservation to give yourselves to each other in marriage?

Will you love and honor each other as man and wife for the rest of your lives?

The following question may be omitted if, for example, the couple is advanced in years.

Will you accept children lovingly from God, and bring them up according to the law of Christ and his Church?

Each answers the questions separately.

Rite of Marriage

Jewish Ceremony

The rabbi addresses the groom:

Do you, _____, take _____ to be your wife, promising to cherish and protect her, whether in good fortune or in adversity, and to seek together with her a life hallowed by the faith of Israel?

The groom answers:

I do.

The rabbi addresses the bride:

Do you, _____, take _____ to be your husband, promising to cherish and protect him, whether in good fortune or in adversity, and to seek together with him a life hallowed by the faith of Israel?

The bride answers:

I do.   *Rabbi's Manual*

Contemporary Ceremony

The officiant asks the groom:

_____, do you come before this gathering of friends and family to proclaim your love and devotion for _____? Do you promise to affirm her, respect her, and care for her during times of joy and hardship? Do you commit yourself to share your feelings of happiness and sadness? Do you pledge to remain faithful to her?

The groom answers:

I do.

The officiant asks the bride:

_____, do you come before this gathering of friends and family to proclaim your love and devotion for _____? Do you promise to affirm him, respect him, and care for him during times of joy and hardship? Do you commit yourself to share your feelings of happiness and sadness? Do you pledge to remain faithful to him?

The bride answers:

I do.   Roger Fritts

. . .

The officiant says to the bride: _____, are you ready for marriage
to _____?
Bride: I am.
The officiant says to the groom: _____, are you ready for marriage
to _____?
Groom: I am.
Officiant: Who is the bride's witness to these vows?
The witness gives his or her name in reply.
Officiant: Who is the groom's witness to these vows?
The witness gives his or her name in reply.

David Hostetter

. . .

The officiant addresses the bride:

_____, will you take this man to be your husband, to live
together according to the best ethical principles? Will you love him,
comfort him in pain and in sorrow? Will you share joy with him when
he is happy and respect his dignity as a man, from this day forward,
forsaking all others?

The officiant addresses the groom:

_____, will you take this woman to be your wife, to live
together according to the best ethical principles? Will you love her,
comfort her in pain and in sorrow? Will you share joy with her when
she is happy and respect her dignity as a woman, from this day forward, forsaking all others?

Paul E. Killinger

Chapter 5

The Vows

*"And Thereto
I Plight Thee My Troth"*

The young couple sitting with me in my office were sixth generation New England Yankees. Deeply committed to tradition, the groom had spent years restoring old New England buildings and cobblestone streets. They requested that I conduct their wedding service using the older text of the *Book of Common Prayer* with its thous and thees. However, the groom had a question about the vows. "What does 'troth' mean? I don't want to promise something when I don't even know what the word means. I am not even sure how to say it."

"It's an old English word that refers to fidelity," I explained. "Although one common pronunciation is a short o, this makes me think of a water trough. In wedding services I prefer to use a long o, the way we do when we pronounce betroth. The word troth has the same root as the word truth. You are promising to be true, to be faithful." The young man thought for a moment. "It applies," he said. "Leave it in."

The question of intent addresses the commitment you each make to society. You face the officiant, who represents the community. You promise to do your best to maintain a stable marriage. You pledge to take responsibility to care for each other and for any children you may have. In contrast, vows are the statements of commitment you make to each other. The clergy and congregation are witnesses. However, you are not speaking to us. You

are addressing each other. You turn and face each other, look each other in the eye, and say your vows.

The vows are the core of the Protestant and Roman Catholic services. You can do without all the other parts of the service, but you must say vows to each other to be married. Couples are more likely to write their own vows than any other part of the service.

There is no single perfect or correct vow for everyone. You can have a wonderful wedding using a traditional vow or by writing your own vows. Don't let anyone intimidate you by insisting that only the most traditional vow is in good taste. Don't believe persons who insist that couples who really love each other always write their own vows. Relax and trust your own judgment. The vows that feel right to the two of you are the right vows for your wedding.

Protestant Ceremony

The groom, facing the bride and taking her right hand in his, says:

In the Name of God, I _____ take you, _____ to be my wife, to have and to hold from this day forward, for better for worse, for richer for poorer, in sickness and in health, to love and to cherish, until we are parted by death. This is my solemn vow.

Then they loose their hands, and the bride, still facing the groom, takes his right hand in hers, and says:

In the Name of God, I _____ take you, _____ to be my husband, to have and to hold from this day forward, for better for worse, for richer for poorer, in sickness and in health, to love and to cherish, until we are parted by death. This is my solemn vow.

They loose their hands.

Book of Common Prayer

The Basic Parts of a Traditional Wedding Ceremony

Roman Catholic Ceremony

Priest: Since it is your intention to enter into marriage, join your right hands, and declare your consent before God and his Church.

They join hands. The groom says:

I, _____, take you, _____, to be my wife. I promise to be true to you in good times and in bad, in sickness and in health. I will love you and honor you all the days of my life.

The bride says:

I, _____, take you, _____, to be my husband. I promise to be true to you in good times and in bad, in sickness and in health. I will love you and honor you all the days of my life.

If, however, it seems preferable for pastoral reasons, the priest may obtain consent from the couple through questions. First he asks the bridegroom:

_____, do you take _____ for your wife? Do you promise to be true to her in good times and in bad, in sickness and in health, to love her and honor her all the days of your life?

The groom: I do.

Then he asks the bride:

_____, do you take _____ for your husband? Do you promise to be true to him in good times and in bad, in sickness and in health, to love him and honor him all the days of your life?

The bride: I do.

Rite of Marriage

Jewish Ceremony

Traditionally there are no marriage vows in a Jewish wedding. However, the bride and groom sometimes say the following words after the exchange of rings. They are from Hosea 2:21:22.

The groom says: I betroth you to me forever; I betroth you to me with steadfast love and compassion, I betroth you to me in faithfulness.

The bride says: I betroth you to me forever; I betroth you to me with steadfast love and compassion, I betroth you to me in faithfulness.   *Rabbi's Manual*

Contemporary Ceremony

The officiant says to the groom: _____, will you look into _____ 's eyes, and into her heart, and repeat after me?

Groom: I commit my life to our partnership in marriage. I promise to comfort you, to encourage you in all walks of life. I promise to express my thoughts and emotions to you, and to listen to you in times of joy and in times of sorrow. _____, I love you, and you are my closest friend. Will you let me share my life and all that I am with you?

Bride: I will.

The officiant says to the bride: _____, will you look into _____ 's eyes, and into his heart, and repeat after me?

Bride: I commit my life to our partnership in marriage. I promise to comfort you, to encourage you in all walks of life. I promise to express my thoughts and emotions to you, and to listen to you in times of joy and in times of sorrow. _____, I love you, and you are my closest friend. Will you let me share my life and all that I am with you?

Groom: I will.   Michael Barlow-Sparkman

• • •

The officiant says to the groom: _____, how do you pledge your love?

Groom: _____, I promise to give you my love, to accept and cherish your love, to help you when you need me. I promise to be your faithful husband in joy and in sorrow, and in sickness and in health.

The officiant says to the bride: _____, how do you pledge your love?

Bride: _____, I promise to give you my love, to accept and cherish your love, to help you when you need me. I promise to be your faithful wife in joy and in sorrow, and in sickness and in health.

John Corrado

• • •

These words are spoken first by the groom and then by the bride:

I promise to be your lover, companion and friend,
Your partner in parenthood,
Your ally in conflict,
Your greatest fan and your toughest adversary.
Your comrade in adventure,
Your student and your teacher,
Your consolation in disappointment,
Your accomplice in mischief,
Your strength in your need and
Vulnerable to you in my own,
And most of all,
Your associate in the search for enlightenment.

Wedding of David Friedman and Robin Colpitts Friedman

• • •

Groom: Mary, I met you nearly three years ago. I remember sitting next to you that first day in class. I sat next to you because I thought you were so beautiful. We talked and became friends. It took me over a year to get the courage to ask you out on a date. You seemed so wonderful, and I was shy. After a few weeks of dating I became convinced that you were the most wonderful person I had ever met and that I could not imagine being without you. As you began to tell me how much you cared about me, I started to develop a confidence in our relationship. I felt a trust that we loved each other deeply, and we could count on each other.

Still, it was difficult for me to make the decision to get married. Getting married means giving up some of my independence. I have enjoyed living alone in my own home, knowing that I could leave my things anywhere I wanted. I have enjoyed knowing I would not interfere with anyone else. Yet there came a time a few months ago when I realized I wanted to make a commitment to you. I want to share the joys and responsibilities and stress of life with you. When you are sick I want to care for you and I want you to care for me when I am ill. I want to share the same house with you. I want to share the same experiences with you so that in twenty or thirty or forty years I can say, "Remember that job I had? Remember that trip we took? Remember that friend we had?" You will say, "Yes, I remember." Most important, I want to have children with you. Mary, I pledge to you my love and caring and fidelity. It will be a joy and an honor to share the rest of my life with you.

Bride: John, I remember when we first met, when we first talked, when you first asked me out. I never thought that I might marry you. I remember thinking of you as an interesting person. After we had been going out together for several weeks, you went home for Christmas vacation to visit your parents. That was an important trip for me, because I realized when you were gone how much I missed you, how much I needed you. I remember going to the airport to greet you when you returned. When I saw you I melted inside and I said to myself that I did not want to be separated from you again. For several months I was completely dependent on you emotionally. It was a wonderful romantic time of poetry, wine and flowers. However, it was also a time when I

was afraid. Occasionally, a fear would grip me that you might suddenly disappear. Gradually that feeling began to fade. Over time I began to trust you and trust myself. Self-confidence grew inside me. I know from experience that I can count on myself and we can count on each other.

John, I want to spend my life with you. I am as sure of this as I have ever been sure of anything. I don't know what the future holds. No doubt there will be times when things will go well for us. There will be other times when one of us will be out of work or ill, or when the world around us will be in chaos. With you, John, I want to share all this. Most important, I want to have children with you. To have a family with you is my wish. John, I pledge to you my love and my fidelity as your wife. I promise to share the rest of my life with you.

Roger Fritts

• • •

Groom: I promise you _____, that I will be your loving and loyal husband from now on and I will share with you all of life's joy and sorrow, pleasure and pain, until death parts us.

Bride: I promise you _____, that I will be your loving and loyal wife from now on and I will share with you all of life's joy and sorrow, pleasure and pain, until death parts us.

David Hostetter

• • •

Groom: I, _____, take you, _____, just as you are, above all others, to share my life.

Bride: I, _____, take you, _____, just as you are, above all others, to share my life.

Angeline E. M. Theisen

Chapter 6
The Rings

"With This Ring I Thee Wed . . ."

Not all couples exchange rings. For example, I officiated at a West Coast outdoor wedding without rings. "We don't want to have rings," the groom explained. "However," said the bride, "I do want to give a gift to Bill after the vows. It will be a surprise."

They held their service at sunrise on the grounds of an old mansion overlooking the Pacific Ocean. After the vows, I turned to the bride and said, "At this time Mary wishes to give Bill a gift."

From the large loose sleeves of her dress Mary carefully removed a small coconut. "Bill, I give you this as a symbol of our relationship. Though hard and rough on the outside, inside there is a soft white layer, sweet and good to eat. In the middle there is a clear liquid, moving, the shape always changing, hard to see, but there at the core, at the center. Our relationship is sometimes hard and rough on the outside. But just below the surface our love is soft, and yielding. It is sweet and physical. However, this is not the center of our relationship. The center of our love is a mystery, moving, changing, but always there."

This gift exchange was different. Imagine the setting: at sunrise overlooking the ocean, with the sights and smells of the sea all around us, the sound of the waves and gulls in the distance, the deep blue sky with the pink of the clouds in the east, and the dark eyes of the bride looking at the groom. They were two young people living life, for a time at least, out of the mainstream, away from tradition. They treated each other with laughter and humor, and with love and respect. I found the service deeply moving. It is

good to be serious about the commitments we make at a wedding, but it is also good to laugh and have fun.

Some historians say that in the past, a wedding ring symbolized ownership of a woman by a man. Others suggest the gold band is a symbol of an ancient tradition of the groom giving the bride a gift of something of value. This valuable gift, such as silver or gold, gave the bride a degree of financial empowerment. Traditional Jewish law requires that, for the marriage to be legal, the groom give something of value to the bride, to "acquire" her. In the Jewish tradition a simple band without decoration or precious stones became the common gift. This is so the ring will not become a symbol of status or economic differences between people.

Today in weddings, rings are gifts and they are also much more. They are the lasting symbols of the vows and commitments made on the wedding day. Long after the cake and flowers are gone and the clothing put away, the ring will remain as a reminder of the promises of the wedding service.

Until the end of the sixteenth century, it was customary for women in England to wear their wedding rings on the third finger of the right hand. Some Catholics still do this. The ancient Egyptians believed that a nerve ran from this finger to the heart. In the Jewish service the traditional ring finger is the index finger of the right hand. Ancient Jews believed a special vein connected this finger directly to the heart. The modern Jewish practice is to place the ring on the finger the wearer plans to wear it on. Today most married persons generally wear the ring on the third finger of the left hand. This follows the practice of ancient Romans who believed a vein in this finger went directly to the heart.

The bride and groom should decide together whether to have a double- or single-ring ceremony. Double-ring ceremonies, where the bride also gives a ring to the groom, began in Europe and became common in America after the Second World War. A few men still prefer not to wear a ring, claiming that they find it uncomfortable, or that they feel awkward wearing jewelry. Women point out this practice is unequal. A wife wears the symbol of marriage and commitment, but the husband does not. Many women today will insist that both the husband and the wife wear a ring.

The exchange of rings is often the point in the service when the congregation, the couple and the officiant laugh. Laughter arises from the feeling of joy and the release of tension that comes after the exchange of vows.

The laughter also comes from the fact that it is not always easy to put a well-fitted ring on another person's finger. You don't want to pinch the hand of the person for whom you have just proclaimed your love. However, you do want to get the ring on. One solution is to smile at your partner, grasp his or her finger firmly with one hand and pull, while pushing the ring on with your other hand. A more conservative approach is to push the ring on the finger of your partner only to the knuckle. Your partner finishes the process by moving the ring over the knuckle. If you have trouble with this during the rehearsal, you can always pick up a coconut at a local food store.

Rings do get lost. At an outdoor ceremony, the bride's eight-year-old daughter was the ring bearer. An attendant had tied each ring with a bow knot intended to make it easy to get the rings off by just pulling the string of each ribbon. At some point before the service one bow came undone, and the groom's ring fell off. The minister, the groom and the bride realized this in the middle of the service. The bride reached for the groom's hand, took his class ring from another finger and used it as the wedding band. Afterward, everyone—the bride, the groom and the wedding guests—looked in the grass until someone found the groom's ring. It was a wonderful wedding with an unusual reception. At another wedding, the best man reached out to hand the ring to the minister and missed the minister's hand. The ring fell to the ground, hit the minister's shoe and rolled into the pews of the church. In the first few pews people looked on the floor until they found the ring and handed it back to the minister.

These are not "things going wrong in a wedding service." Nothing can go wrong in a wedding service. You gather to celebrate a relationship between two people, and you can celebrate that relationship even if the ring gets lost or another detail does not go as expected. What matters is the love you have for each other. A wonderful wedding is a wedding where people affirm a relationship, not where people focus on the details. Working out the details can be fun, interesting, satisfying and frustrating, but don't let the details take control of your feelings. If you remember that the goal is to celebrate a relationship, many details can go wrong and you will still have a wonderful wedding.

Protestant Ceremony

Blessing of the Rings

The priest may ask God's blessing on a ring or rings as follows:

> Bless, O Lord, this ring, to be a sign of the vows by which this man and this woman have bound themselves to each other; through Jesus Christ our Lord. Amen.

Exchange of the Rings

The giver places the ring on the ring finger of the other's hand and says:

> _____, I give you this ring as a symbol of my vow, and with all that I am, and all that I have, I honor you, in the Name of the Father, and of the Son, and of the Holy Spirit (or in the Name of God).

Repeat for the second ring.

Book of Common Prayer

Roman Catholic Ceremony

Blessing of the Rings

> *Priest:* May the Lord bless these rings which you give to each other as the sign of your love and fidelity. Amen.

or

Priest: Lord, bless these rings which we bless in your name. Grant that those who wear them may always have a deep faith in each other. May they do your will and always live together in peace, goodwill, and love. We ask this through Christ our Lord. Amen.

or

Priest: Lord, bless and consecrate _____ and _____ in their love for each other. May these rings be a symbol of true faith in each other, and always remind them of their love. Through Christ our Lord. Amen.

Exchange of the Rings

The groom places his wife's ring on her ring finger. He may say:

_____, take this ring as a sign of my love and fidelity. In the name of the Father, and of the Son, and of the Holy Spirit.

The bride places her husband's ring on his ring finger. She may say:

_____, take this ring as a sign of my love and fidelity. In the name of the Father, and of the Son, and of the Holy Spirit.

Rite of Marriage

Jewish Ceremony

Exchange of the Rings

1. *The rabbi says:* _____ and _____, speak the words and exchange the rings that make you husband and wife.

_____, as you place the ring on the finger of the one you love, recite the words that formally unite you in marriage.

Bride and groom face each other and say successively: Be consecrated to me with this ring as my wife/husband in keeping with the heritage of Moses and Israel.

or

Be wedded to me with this ring as my wife/husband in keeping with the religion of the Jewish people.

The rabbi might read the Ketubah *here (see chapter 12).*

2. *The rabbi says to the groom*: Take this ring and, placing it upon the finger of your bride, say to her the words that confirm your covenant of marriage.

The groom says: May you, _____, be consecrated to me by this ring as my wife according to the law of God and the faith of Israel.

The rabbi says to the bride: Take this ring and, placing it upon the finger of your groom, say to him the words that confirm your covenant of marriage.

The bride says: May you, _____, be consecrated to me by this ring as my husband according to the law of God and the faith of Israel.

3. *The rabbi says*: In keeping with the declaration you have made, you give (and you receive) this ring/these rings. It is/they are a token of your union, a symbol of enduring loyalty. May it/they ever remind you that your lives are bound together by devotion and faithfulness.

The rabbi says to the groom: As you, _____, place this ring upon the finger of the bride, speak to her these words, "With this ring be consecrated to me as my wife according to the faith of Moses and Israel."

The rabbi says to the bride: And as you, _____, place this ring upon your bridegroom's finger as a token of wedlock, say to him these words, "With this ring be consecrated to me as my husband according to the faith of Moses and Israel."

Rabbi's Manual

Contemporary Ceremony

Officiant: From the earliest times, the circle has been a symbol of completeness, a symbol of committed love. An unbroken and never ending circle symbolizes a commitment of love that is also never ending. As often as either of you looks at this symbol, I hope that you will be reminded of the commitment to love each other, which you have made today.

Will each of you repeat after me:

Groom: I, _____, give to you _____, this ring, as a symbol of my commitment to love, honor, and respect you.

Bride: I, _____, give to you _____, this ring, as a symbol of my commitment to love, honor, and respect you.

Michael Barlow-Sparkman

• • •

Officiant: What token of your pledge do you offer each other?

As the bride places the ring on the groom's finger she says:

_____, I offer this ring to you as a symbol of my love and of the vows I have spoken. What meaning will it have for you as you wear it?

The groom responds to the question, stating the meaning of the wedding ring to him:

> The ring is a symbol for me and for the community around me that I have made this commitment. It is a sign that I take it very seriously.

As the groom places the ring on the bride's finger he says:

> _____, I offer this ring to you as a symbol of my love and of the vows I have just spoken. What meaning will it have for you as you wear it?

The bride responds to the question, stating the meaning of the wedding ring to her:

> We looked for the perfect ring for a long time. As I wear this ring, it will remind me that you and I will be together for a long time. I will remember that when I am struggling, you will struggle with me. When I rejoice, you will rejoice with me. When you struggle, I will struggle with you and when you rejoice, I will rejoice with you.
>
> Laurinda Bilyeu and Stephen Weiser

•   •   •

Officiant: The rings you give and receive this day are the symbols of the endless love into which you enter as husband and wife. Such a love has no beginning and no ending, no giver and no receiver. You are each the beginning and the ending, each the giver and the receiver.

Groom: I give this ring in remembrance of this hour, a symbol of love that is complete, beautiful and endless.

Bride: I give this ring in remembrance of this hour, a symbol of love that is complete, beautiful and endless.

John Corrado

Blessing of the Ring

The officiant says:

May I have the bride's ring, please?

Holding the bride's ring in the palm of his or her hand, the officiant says a blessing:

The circle is the symbol of the sun and the earth and the universe. It is a symbol of holiness and of perfection and of peace. This ring is a symbol of unity, in which your two lives are now joined in one unbroken circle. _____, please place this ring on _____'s finger and repeat after me:

Exchange of the Rings

The groom says: I give you this ring to wear upon your hand as a symbol of our unity.

Blessing of the Ring

The officiant says:

May I have the groom's ring please?

Holding the groom's ring in the palm of his or her hand, the officiant repeats the blessing:

The circle is the symbol of the sun and the earth and the universe. It is a symbol of holiness and of perfection and of peace. This ring is a symbol of unity, in which your two lives are now joined in one unbroken circle. _____, please place this ring on _____'s finger and repeat after me:

Exchange of the Ring

The bride says: I give you this ring to wear upon your hand as a symbol of our unity.

Kenneth L. Patton

• • •

Groom: May this ring forever be to you the symbol of my growing love.

Bride: May this ring forever be to you the symbol of my growing love.

Angeline E. M. Theisen

• • •

Officiant: You have chosen these rings as the symbol of your marriage covenant. They are made of gold, a metal that does not tarnish and is enduring. These rings represent the ties that bind you together as husband and wife. They are an endless circle representing your marriage union, which shall continue, broken only by death.

Groom: In token and pledge of our constant faith and abiding love, with this ring I marry you.

Bride: In token and pledge of our constant faith and abiding love, with this ring I marry you.

Richard W. Thomas

Chapter 7

The Blessing

"Send Thy Blessing
Upon These Thy Servants"

"*I* want this to be a spiritual service," the bride to be said to me as we sat in my office. "However, Harry doesn't believe in God."

Does God exist? What does the word "God" refer to? How can we define God? Do our lives on this earth have a purpose? How does our marriage fit into this purpose? How does my partner feel about these questions? These are issues that often surface for couples who attempt to compose their own wedding service. They are worth spending time talking about with your partner.

Throughout the wedding service there are opportunities to mention, or not to mention, God. Millions of Americans are sure that God exists. If you fall into this group, you will clearly understand the need for a prayer at this point in the wedding service. The prayer is a request for God to bless this marriage.

On the other hand, millions of Americans do not believe in God. If you fall into this group, you will want something other than a prayer. A request that family and friends bless and support this marriage might feel more appropriate to you.

In the middle are millions of people who believe in God most of the

time, but occasionally have doubts. If you are in this group, you may wish to think about this issue and have a serious talk with your partner before deciding to have a particular blessing.

No matter how you feel about the question of the existence of God, I encourage you to cultivate respect, care, understanding and honesty in relating to people. Open yourself to the beauty of music or a poem. Experience the glory of the earth. I believe, whether or not we are comfortable with the word God, we should attend to our relationships with people, with works of art, and with nature. In these relationships we will find a unity and meaning to life that will give us strength and renewal.

Here are examples of prayers and blessings that can come after the exchange of rings.

Protestant Ceremony

All standing, the celebrant says:

Let us Pray together in the words that our Savior has taught us.

People and celebrant:

Our Father, who art in heaven, hallowed be thy Name, thy kingdom come, thy will be done, on earth as it is in heaven. Give us this day our daily bread. And forgive us our trespasses, as we forgive those who trespass against us. And lead us not into temptation, but deliver us from evil. For thine is the kingdom, and the power, and the glory, for ever and ever. Amen.

The deacon or other person appointed reads the following prayers, to which the people respond, saying, "Amen." If there is not to be a Communion, one or more of the prayers may be omitted.

Let us pray. Eternal God, creator and preserver of all life, author of salvation, and giver of all grace: Look with favor upon the world you have made, and for which your Son gave his life, and especially upon this man and this woman whom you make one flesh in Holy Matrimony. Amen.

Give them wisdom and devotion in the ordering of their common life, that each may be to the other a strength in need, a counselor in perplexity, a comfort in sorrow, and a companion in joy. Amen

Grant that their wills may be so knit together in your will, and their spirits in your Spirit, that they may grow in love and peace with you and one another all the days of their life. Amen.

Give them grace, when they hurt each other, to recognize and acknowledge their fault, and to seek each other's forgiveness and yours. *Amen.*

Make their life together a sign of Christ's love to this sinful and broken world, that unity may overcome estrangement, forgiveness heal guilt, and joy conquer despair. Amen.

Bestow on them, if it is your will, the gift and heritage of children, and the grace to bring them up to know you, to love you, and serve you. Amen.

Give them such fulfillment of their mutual affection that they may reach out in love and concern for others. Amen.

Grant that all married persons who have witnessed these vows may find their lives strengthened and their loyalties confirmed. Amen.

Grant that the bonds of our common humanity, by which all your children are united one to another, and the living to the dead, may be so transformed by your grace, that your will may be done on earth as it is in heaven; where, O Father, with your Son and the Holy Spirit, you live and reign in perfect unity, now and for ever. Amen.

Book of Common Prayer

Roman Catholic Ceremony

In the Rite of Marriage *general intercessions follow the exchange of rings. The intercessions begin with an invitation. One example follows. There are two others in the* Rite of Marriage, *or the priest may use his own words. The priest faces the bride and groom and, with hands joined, says:*

> *Priest:* Now that we have heard God's word in the Bible and felt his presence in this exchange of vows, let us present to God the Father these petitions for people in the world today.

There follows a series of intentions for the couple to which the people respond, usually saying "Lord hear our prayer." Here is one of three suggested forms in the Rite of Marriage:

General Intercessions

> *Reader:* The response is "Lord, hear our prayer." For our Holy Father on earth, the Pope, all the bishops and the clergy everywhere that they may lead us to a deeper faith in God and a stronger love for others, let us pray to the Lord.

> *People:* Lord, hear our prayer.

> *Reader:* For our president and all leaders of government that they may be effective in achieving peace and eliminating poverty, let us pray to the Lord.

> *People:* Lord, hear our prayer.

> *Reader:* For married persons that they may continue to give, be able to forgive and find happiness deepen with the passing of each day, let us pray to the Lord.

> *People:* Lord, hear our prayer.

The Blessing

Reader: For _____ and _____, now beginning their life together, that they may have divine assistance at every moment, the constant support of friends, the rich blessing of children, a warm love reaching out to others and good health until a ripe old age, let us pray to the Lord.

People: Lord, hear our prayer.

Reader: For those who are sick, lonely, discouraged or oppressed that they may be strengthened by God's help and aided by their friends, let us pray to the Lord.

People: Lord, hear our prayer.

Reader: For those who have died, especially the relatives and friends of _____ and _____ and of all present for this wedding, that they may enjoy perfect happiness and total fulfillment in eternal life, let us pray to the Lord.

People: Lord, hear our prayer.

Reader: For these personal needs which we mention now in silence (pause), let us pray to the Lord.

People: Lord, hear our prayer.

Priest: O God our Father in heaven, your Son taught us to ask, to seek and to knock. We have just done so, confident that you will now look upon our many needs, consider our trusting faith, and in your great love grant these requests which we present to you through Jesus Christ our Lord.

People Respond: Amen.

After the intercessions, when the marriage does not take place within the context of a mass, the priest says the nuptial blessing. Besides the examples that follow, there are

two other forms of the nuptial blessing that can be chosen. Words enclosed in the parenthesis are optional:

Holy Father, you created humankind in your own image and made man and woman to be joined as husband and wife in union of body and heart and so fulfill their mission in this world. Father, to reveal the plan of your love, you made the union of husband and wife an image of the covenant between you and your people. In the fulfillment of this sacrament, the marriage of a Christian man and woman is a sign of the marriage between Christ and the Church. Father, stretch out your hand, and bless _____ and _____. Lord, grant that as they begin to live this sacrament they may share with each other the gifts of your love and become one in heart and mind as witnesses to your presence in their marriage. Help them to create a home together (and give them children to be formed by the Gospel and to have a place in your family). Give your blessings to _____, your daughter, so that she may be a good wife (and mother), caring for the home, faithful in love for her husband, generous and kind. Give your blessings to _____, your son, so that he may be a faithful husband (and a good father). Father, grant that as they come together to your table on earth, so they may one day have the joy of sharing your feast in heaven. (We ask this) through Christ our Lord. Amen.

If marriage is celebrated between a Catholic and an unbaptized person, the following form of the nuptial blessing is used. Facing them, the priest joins his hands and says:

My brothers and sisters, let us ask God for his continued blessings upon this bridegroom and his bride.

All pray silently for a short while. Then the priest extends his hands and continues (words in the parenthesis are optional):

Holy Father, creator of the universe, maker of man and woman in your own likeness, source of blessing for the married life, we humbly pray to you for this bride who today is united with her husband in the bond of

marriage. May your fullest blessing come upon her and her husband so that they may together rejoice in your gift of married love. May they be noted for their good lives, (and be parents filled with virtue). Lord, may they both praise you when they are happy and turn to you in their sorrow. May they be glad that you help them in their work, and know that you are with them in their need. May they reach old age in the company of their friends, and come at last to the kingdom of heaven. (We ask this) through Christ our Lord. Amen.

Rite of Marriage

Jewish Ceremony

We praise You, Adonai our God, Ruler of the universe, who hallows us with *mitzvot* and consecrates this marriage. We praise You, Adonai, who sanctifies our people Israel through *kiddushin*, the sacred rite of marriage at the *huppah*.

And now, we recite the seven wedding blessings, the *Sheva Berachot*, praying that God will grant you fulfillment and joy.

We praise You, Adonai our God, Ruler of the universe, who has created all things for Your glory.

We praise You, Adonai our God, Ruler of the universe, Creator of man and woman.

We praise You, Adonai our God, Ruler of the universe, who has fashioned us in Your own image and has established marriage for the fulfillment and perpetuation of life in accordance with Your holy purpose. We praise You, Adonai, Creator of man and woman.

We praise You, Adonai our God, Ruler of the universe, source of all gladness and joy. Through Your grace we attain affection, companion-

ship, and peace. Grant that the love that unites this bridegroom and bride may gladden their souls. May their family life be ennobled through their devotion to the faith of Israel. May there be peace in their home, quietness and confidence in their hearts. May they be sustained by Your comforting presence in the midst of our people, and by the promise of salvation for all humanity. We praise You, Adonai our God, who unites bridegroom and bride in holy joy.

Rabbi's Manual

Contemporary Ceremony

_____ and _____, may the warmth of your love melt the snows of all your barriers, and may you truly be united as one, spiritually, emotionally and physically. Your parents, your families and your friends now recognize your commitment. Let us pray.

Most holy God, mother and father of all creation, may your blessings continue for _____ and _____. May you encourage and help each of them to develop into a more complete person, by becoming a more united couple. May the living spirit of Jesus grant them patience to mend their differences, wisdom and guidance in all their decisions. May the spirit of Jesus grant them grace in times of disappointment, and peace that comforts them all the days of their lives. We pray these things, believing in the power and the everlasting love of Jesus. Amen.

Michael Barlow-Sparkman

• • •

The officiant speaks first to the congregation of its responsibilities:

This is a moment of celebration. Let it also be a moment of dedication. The world does a good job of reminding us of how fragile we are. Individuals are fragile; relationships are fragile, too. Every marriage needs the love, nurture and support of a network of friends and family. On

this wedding day I ask you not only to be friends of _____ or _____ but friends of _____ and _____ together, friends of the relationship.

In the moment of silence that follows, I ask each of you, in your own way, to confer a silent prayer, blessing, wish or hope upon this wedding.

The officiant pauses for a moment of silence.

Blessing:

May the love you have found grow in meaning and strength until its beauty is shown in a common devotion to all that is compassionate and life-giving. May the flow of your love help brighten the face of the earth. May the source of all love touch and bless us and grace our lives with color and courage.

John Corrado

• • •

Creator, Savior, Loving Spirit, bless this couple who have committed themselves to each other in marriage and have come seeking your benediction. Surrounded by their families and friends, may they feel encircled by your love as well as theirs. Assure them of your presence in days of joy like this one and in days of sorrow, pain and bereavement. Strengthen their relationship through all the tests of adversity and brighten it with a generous measure of happiness.

Help them make their home a place where they love children and welcome friends. Spare them from interference by those who through wanting to help may intrude in what are the proper responsibilities of husband and wife, father and mother and children.

Make them good neighbors, doing for others what they would have others do for them.

Teach us all to love each other as we love ourselves and to love you with all our heart and strength and mind. Hear these our prayers. Amen.

David Hostetter

• • •

_____ and _____ —as a collection of words, this ceremony would count for little, were it not for the love and commitment which you here pledge to one another. By virtue of being human, there is distance between you, which is both infinite and infinitesimal, at one and the same time. Today you have joined in a covenant bridging that distance. Always remember that in reaching across any distance, you are faced with two choices: to circle the globe in one direction or to take one step in the other. May you ever seek the shorter distance, for love is as difficult—and as simple—as that.

Fred F. Keip

• • •

_____ and _____, you have now affirmed before your families and friends your love and your caring for each other. You have come from different backgrounds. You have walked different paths. You are different individuals. Your love has transcended these differences. In the years before you may the richness of the traditions that have nurtured you enhance and brighten your lives as you help to create and shape the future.

May the challenges of your life together be met with courage and optimism. May you learn from your failures and grow in your achievements. May life bless you with children, friends and family in a wide network of mutual support and enjoyment. May you face pain, toil and trouble with a stout but light heart. May you share with others the radiance of your seasons of joy and pleasure. May you always remember that laughter is the medicine of the gods.

May the spirit of love be ever a part of your lives so that the union we here celebrate this day be worthy of continued celebration tomorrow and tomorrow and tomorrow.

Kenneth W. Phifer

• • •

Most gracious God: We thank you for the beauty of this moment. Send your richest blessing upon _____ and _____, whom we bless in your name, that they may love, honor, and cherish each other, amid the ever-changing scenes of this life. Look favorably upon them, that their home may be a haven of blessing and a place of peace. Grant them fullness of years so that they may see their children's children. Guide them by the wise counsel of your word, and when their earthly life is complete, give them entrance into your everlasting kingdom. And now . . .

> May God bless you and keep you.
> May God's presence shine upon you
> and be gracious to you.
> May God's presence be with you and
> Give you peace.
>   Amen.

Richard W. Thomas

Chapter 8

The Announcement or Declaration

"Forasmuch as . . ."

"I don't want any pronouncement," explained a young man. "A pronouncement suggests that from up high you have studied our relationship. It implies that you have evaluated our characters and reviewed the commitments we have made to each other. It suggests that you have passed judgment on us, decided to give us permission to be married. However, you have not looked at our relationship in that way and we would not want you to pass judgment on us. In truth, you cannot marry us. Only we can marry each other."

I encounter this point of view occasionally. From watching movies or television, many people have in their minds the words "by the power vested in me by the church and the state I now pronounce you husband and wife." (Even worse is "man and wife." This phrase puts the couple on unequal footing. The identity of the man remains the same, but the officiant suddenly transforms the identity of the woman and defines her by her relationship to the man. The phrase is no longer a part of most wedding services.)

Today most announcements or declarations do not include the words "by the power vested in me . . ." Most are simply descriptions by clergy of what has happened during the exchange of vows and rings. These descriptions are not ritualized passings of judgment on relationships. They are ceremonial ways of summarizing and affirming what has just occurred.

The Announcement or Declaration

Protestant Ceremony

In the Book of Common Prayer *the following announcement comes after the exchange of rings in chapter 6 and before the blessing in chapter 7.*

Then the celebrant joins the right hand of husband and wife and says:

Now that _____ and _____ have given themselves to each other by solemn vows, with the joining of hands and the giving and receiving of a *ring*, I pronounce that they are husband and wife, in the Name of the Father, and of the Son, and of the Holy Spirit.

Those whom God has joined together let no one put asunder.

People: Amen.

Book of Common Prayer

Roman Catholic Ceremony

In the Rite of Marriage *the declaration of the marriage comes after the exchange of vows in chapter 5 and before the exchange of rings in chapter 6. Receiving their consent, the priest says:*

You have declared your consent before the Church. May the Lord in his goodness strengthen your consent and fill you both with his blessings.

What God has joined, men must not divide.

Response: Amen.

Rite of Marriage

Jewish Ceremony

In the presence of these witnesses and in keeping with our tradition, you have spoken the words and performed the rites that unite your lives.

_____ and _____, you are now husband and wife in the sight of God, the Jewish community, and all people. I ask you and all who are gathered here to pray in silence, seeking God's blessings upon your marriage and your home.

Rabbi's Manual

Contemporary Ceremony

I present to you, _____ and _____, equal partners, husband and wife, united in holy matrimony.

Michael Barlow-Sparkman

• • •

_____ and _____ have vowed their love in our presence. We now recognize them as husband and wife.

John Corrado

• • •

Before this gathering _____ and _____ have promised each other their love and have given each other rings to wear as a sign of their deep commitment. Therefore I declare that they are husband and wife.

Roger Fritts

• • •

Officiant: As you have heard, _____ and _____ have made their wedding vows and exchanged rings as a covenant of their

new relationship. We now declare that they are husband and wife in the name of God, one God for us all, for all time. Amen.

Now let all who rejoice in their wedding say after me: God bless them! *Congregation*: God bless them!

David Hostetter

• • •

The following is meant to be read in unison by the bride and groom, facing the assembly.

Because we have grown in knowledge and love for one another; because we agree in our desire to go forward into life seeking a richer and ever deepening relationship; and because we have pledged ourselves to meet sorrow and joy as one family, we affirm that we are now husband and wife.

The minister shall confirm their statement as follows:

Because they have so affirmed, in love and knowledge one of the other, so also do I declare that _____ and _____ are now husband and wife.

Paul E. Killinger

Chapter 9

The Closing Words

"Bless, Preserve, and Keep You"

$\mathscr{I}$ stood before the couple in the church. She was about to explode with excitement. He was beaming. I was smiling. After I came to the end of the service and said, "Congratulations!" The bride smiled at me and reached over and kissed me (not the groom) full on the lips! She then turned and kissed the groom.

Later she apologized for kissing me before her new husband. "I am so embarrassed," she said.

"Don't be," I said. "It happens all the time." Actually this does not happen all the time. However, it was nice that she wanted to thank me. Remember, as I said in chapter 6, nothing can go wrong in a wedding. We gather to celebrate a relationship. We can celebrate that relationship even when some details do not go as planned.

The words you pick for the ending of the service, like all the service, depend on personal preference. There is no one right way to end. Here are some examples of what are variously called closing words, closing blessings, closing prayers or benedictions.

Protestant Ceremony

The people remain standing. The husband and wife kneel, and the priest says one of the following prayers:

Most gracious God, we give you thanks for your tender love in sending

Jesus Christ to come among us, to be born of a human mother, and to make the way of the cross to be the way of life. We thank you, also, for consecrating the union of man and woman in his Name. By the power of your Holy Spirit, pour out the abundance of your blessing upon this man and woman. Defend them from every enemy. Lead them into all peace. Let their love for each other be a seal upon their hearts, a mantle about their shoulders, and a crown upon their foreheads. Bless them in their work and in their companionship; in their sleeping and in their waking; in their joys and in their sorrows; in their life and in their death. Finally, in your mercy, bring them to that table where your saints feast forever in your heavenly home; through Jesus Christ our Lord, who with you and the Holy Spirit lives and reigns, one God, forever and ever. Amen.

or this:

O God, you have so consecrated the covenant of marriage that in it is represented the spiritual unity between Christ and his Church: Send therefore your blessing upon these your servants, that they may so love, honor, and cherish each other in faithfulness and patience, in wisdom and true godliness, that their home may be a haven of blessing and peace; through Jesus Christ our Lord, who lives and reigns with you and the Holy Spirit, one God, now and forever. Amen.

The husband and wife still kneeling, the priest adds this blessing:

God the Father, God the Son, God the Holy Spirit, bless, preserve, and keep you; the Lord mercifully with his favor look upon you, and fill you with all spiritual benediction and grace; that you may faithfully live together in this life, and in the age to come have life everlasting. Amen.

The Peace

The celebrant may say to the people:

The peace of the Lord be always with you.

People: And also with you.

The newly married couple then greet each other, after which greetings may be exchanged throughout the congregation.

When Communion is not to follow, the wedding party leaves the church. A hymn, psalm or anthem may be sung, or instrumental music may be played.

Book of Common Prayer

Roman Catholic Ceremony

The marriage rite concludes with the recitation of the Lord's Prayer by all present and the blessing. The Rite of Marriage *includes four blessings that the priest may use. Below is one example. The priest may also use the simple form of blessing:* "May almighty God bless you, the Father and the Son and the Holy Spirit." *The people respond* "Amen."

> May God, the almighty Father,
> give you his joy
> and bless you (in your children).

People: Amen.

> May the only Son of God have mercy on you
> and help you in good times and in bad.

People: Amen.

May the Holy Spirit of God
always fill your hearts with his love.

People: Amen.

And may almighty God bless you all,
the Father, and the Son, and the Holy Spirit.

People: Amen

Rite of Marriage

Jewish Ceremony

May God bless you and keep you.
May God's presence shine upon you and be gracious to you.
May God's presence be with you and give you peace.

Rabbi's Manual

Contemporary Ceremony

Now you will feel no rain, for each of you will be shelter to the
other.
Now you will feel no cold, for each of you will be warmth to the
other.
Now you will feel no loneliness, for each of you will be a
companion to the other.
Now you are two bodies, but there is only one life before you.
Go now to your dwelling place, to enter the days of your life
together.
And may your days be good, and long upon the earth.

Adapted from an Apache wedding prayer

Now may you depart in peace,
May your love cast out small fears,
May your hope endure.
May your faith in each other
      and in this radiant universe in
      which the mystery of love happens
      grow and flourish. Amen.

From *To Love Honor and Shave Twice a Week,*
David A. Johnson

• • •

Out of this tangled world two souls have come together, drawn by mutual love and respect. May their days and years yet unborn deepen the joy of their choice and make it abidingly true.

From *To Love Honor and Shave Twice a Week,*
David A. Johnson

• • •

By your free choice you have made a marriage.
No matter what the demands on your
      lives and your time,
The meaning of your living is now
      known through your love.
You must nurture each other to fullness
      and wholeness, renew yourselves
      in love and laughter, maintain the
capacity for wonder, spontaneity,
humor, sensitivity, and save time for
each other, to love each other more
deeply and learn to love more fully
the Creation in which the mystery of
love happens. Amen.

From *To Love Honor and Shave Twice a Week,*
David A. Johnson

• • •

You are now wed.
May you always remain sweethearts, helpmates and
    friends.
May your life together be full of kindness and
    understanding, thoughtfulness and rejoicing.
May the years bring you happiness and contentment.
May you enter into each other's sorrow by sympathy,
Into each other's joy with gladness,
Into each other's hope with faith and trust,
Into each other's need with the sure presence of love,
Into each other's lives with enthusiasm and embracing. Amen.

From *To Love Honor and Shave Twice a Week*,
David A. Johnson

• • •

May these two find happiness in their union. May they live faithfully together, performing the vow and covenant they have made between them; and may they ever remain in sympathy and understanding: that their years may be rich in the joys of life, and their days good, and long upon the earth.

Kenneth L. Patton

• • •

May this moment gleam eternally in your lives. May it add glory to every achievement and cast a blessed light over any ill fortune that may appear. May you give vitality to each other in all undertakings. May you care for each other in all sadness. May you give cheer to each other as you each care for the sacred passion of love. May all that is virtuous, beautiful and trustworthy, remain with you always. Amen.

Roger Fritts

Variations Within the

Basic Service

Chapter 10

The Inclusion of the Family

The Involvement of the Parents

"I have a problem," said the young woman. "My father has his heart set on walking to the altar with me and standing next to me at the beginning of the service. He wants the minister to say, 'Who gives this woman to be married to this man?' so that he can say, 'I do.'

"I love my father, but I just cannot stand the thought of him giving me away. That part of the service says that I am a possession, an object, a commodity being given by one man to another. No one should 'give' a person away or 'receive' a person as a gift. I want everyone in my wedding service to be treated equally, with respect, including me."

This is a concern with which I understand and agree. To acknowledge the mutual love and pride the parents and the bride and groom feel toward each other can be a deeply moving part of a wedding service. However, there needs to be ways to do this that do not imply ownership of women by men. There are several alternatives to the traditional "giving away of the bride."

The *Book of Common Prayer* offers the option of involving the parents after the question of intent and before the reading. As an alternative to the traditional giving away of the bride, it suggests the following wording. It is inclusive of all the parents, not just the father of the bride.

Officiant: Who presents this woman and this man to be married to each other?

To this question, both the parents of the bride and the parents of the groom answer together: "We do."

Book of Common Prayer

• • •

A second alternative is a question that invites the parents to give their blessing to the marriage. Here is an example.

Officiant: Though we go forth from the homes of our childhood, we never outgrow the special love and support of our parents.

To the parents: Do you give the blessing of parents upon _____ and _____? Will you honor the covenant into which your children enter today, give them your loving support, and respect the threshold of their new home?

The parents respond: We will.

Kendyl Gibbons

• • •

A third alternative to the tradition of giving away the bride is for each parent to write a short letter to the couple. The letter expresses their hopes for their children's future. The parents or the officiant can publicly read the letters during the service. If the parents intend the letters to be private, they can present them to the bride and groom, who can read them after the service. Here are two examples:

From a Father

Dear son,

I don't have all the answers. I feel things more than I know things. I married your mother because I loved her, and I felt strongly that it was

the right thing to do. That feeling has stayed with me for more than twenty years. As your father over these many years I have done my best more by feeling than by reason. It felt right to hold you close to me when you were young, to hug you and hold you each night as you were falling to sleep. It felt right to be honest with you when you asked questions, to tell you I was sorry when I felt that I had made a mistake. It felt right to push you to take responsibility for your life when you were old enough to handle it.

Today this marriage of yours feels right to me. It is more than the fact that you and Sharon have fun together, or that you share many interests and values. These things are important, but your relationship feels right to me at a much deeper level. It is a feeling that I cannot explain in words.

You both have my blessing, my support and my love. My only advice is; trust your feelings. May God continue to bless you and our family.

Sincerely,
Your father

From a Mother

Dear daughter,

This wedding, and your new relationship, is wonderful. You both have my love and support. After more than twenty years of marriage and work and children, I have learned what works for me in my marriage. I have found that honesty always works best. I have found that fidelity to your father is the only way I can live. I have found that a sense of humor is essential for my survival. I have found that life is shorter than we realize. Therefore I need to make time for the things I enjoy the most; time to share a joke, or watch a sunset, or make love with your father. My wish, my hope, is that working together in this busy world you can separate the trivial from what is really important. In being true to what is important, may you find joy and happiness.

Love,
Your mother

A fourth alternative to the giving away of the bride is a gift of flowers from the bride and groom to their parents, following the question of intent. This is particularly effective in interfaith marriages. Flowers are not associated with a particular religious belief and can be used to reach out to parents and grandparents of different religious backgrounds. Here are two examples.

Officiant: As they come before us to be married, _____ and _____ wish to acknowledge and thank (bride's parents' names) and (groom's parents' names) for the love and support they have given them. The flowers they give to their parents represent feelings of gratitude in the hearts of _____ and _____. This moment marks a major change in their lives, but the ties of love and friendship with their parents will continue.

The bride and groom then walk to their parents, who rise, and the bride and groom hug each of them and give each a rose.

Roger Fritts

. . .

Officiant: _____ and _____, as you share a rose with your parents, let this be a symbol of your love for each other's relatives. Marriage is more than simply the joining of two lives. It is the marriage of two families. May your love for them, as well as their love for you, live on, by God's grace.

The bride and groom give each set of parents a rose.

Richard W. Thomas

. . .

Another way to include parents in the service is to ask them to pledge their support following the exchange of vows and rings. Here is an example, which goes on to include the entire congregation.

Officiant: Will the parents of _____ and _____ please rise, and before God and all who are gathered here, affirm your blessings, support and encouragement. I remind you that, although each of them will remain a part of your separate heritage, they are no longer

your separate children. _____ and _____ are here, before Almighty God, to become one. Therefore, I now ask you: do you offer your blessings and loving support of this marriage?

Parents: I do.

I now ask everyone to rise. Do all of you gathered here today also pledge your support and encouragement for the commitment that _____ and _____ have made to one another? If so you pledge, would each of you respond by saying I do.

Congregation responds: I do.

Michael Barlow-Sparkman

. . .

Sometimes a parent is unable to be present, or there is a divorce and both a natural parent and a stepparent are present. One way I have seen this handled is for the bride and groom to approach the parents and stepparent before the first words are spoken. They give each a hug and a flower, leaving out the words above. The lack of words adds ambiguity to the situation, which makes it easier to be inclusive of everyone present.

Sometimes one or both parents have died. You may want to include a reference to the deceased by having the officiant say a few words.

Officiant: As we celebrate this wedding today, we honor the memory of _____, the mother of _____. She is with us today in our hearts. The love that she gave _____ lives on in the love that _____ brings to this marriage.

There are movies that portray the father of the bride as doubtful about his daughter's wedding and highly competitive with his new son-in-law and his new in-laws. At one wedding I met a man who was handing out small preprinted cards. The card read "I am the father of the bride. Nobody's paying much attention to me today. But I can assure you, that I am getting my share of attention, for the banks and several business firms are watching me very closely."

I question this stereotype of the bride's father. Most are not pathetic males, who are ignored by the rest of the family and forced to pay large sums of money for a wedding they are ambivalent about. In my experience such cliche views of the bride's father are the exception, not the rule. However, I do believe you can never go wrong in singling out parents for special thanks and appreciation.

The Inclusion of Children from Another Marriage

Because of death or divorce, sometimes there are children from another marriage. There are many ways that they can be included in the wedding. A great deal depends on the age of the children. Couples often ask younger children to be ring bearers or flower girls and to stand next to their parent during the service or sit in the front row.

I have seen the mother or father of the children turn to them before the vows and exchange of rings and speak to them about the new relationship. This can be deeply moving. Here is an example of a mother addressing her five-year-old son:

Bride: Kevin, as my son you are special in my life. We are here to celebrate a new relationship between John and me, and to recognize and celebrate the beginning of a new family relationship. Kevin, one reason I decided to marry John is that he cares so deeply for you as well as for me. I also decided to marry him because I need help. Kevin, you have questions about life for which I don't always have good answers. You need care, concern and understanding and I am not always able to meet your needs. John can help with these things. John is joining our family because together we will all have a richer, deeper, more satisfying life.

I have also seen the new stepparent address the children. Here is an example of an address to a seven-year-old and a nine-year-old.

Groom: Sally and Jill, I am looking forward to sharing a home with you because I find you both to be wonderfully interesting and exciting. For my part, I pledge to you that I will work hard to learn the ways of your family, to understand your needs and interests, your likes and dislikes. I promise that I will share with your mother the responsibility of caring for you and nurturing you so that you will grow to become mature independent adults. Sally and Jill, I love you, and I look forward to our relationship together.

Here is an example of a stepparent addressing his new responsibilities. It is a composite of writings by two persons. The children are ages seven and eleven.

Officiant: There are children who will share in this marriage. The gathering of this new family will deeply influence their lives. It will both complicate and enrich their lives. They also will have much to contribute to this new family.

This ceremony marks not only the union of Dave and Kerry as husband and wife, it also celebrates the combining of Dave with Kerry and her children, Amanda and David, to form a new family.

Dave, have you given serious and unhurried consideration to your role in and responsibility for this family?

Groom answers: Yes.

Is it your intention to be protector, provider, mentor, teacher, companion, and friend of Amanda and David? Do you commit yourself to be an example for them by the way you lead your life? With Kerry and with their father, do you promise to raise them to be responsible members of society?

Groom answers: I do.

We pray that this man and woman, and this newly created family, will weave together a fabric of mutual consolation and support, of challenge

and help. May they develop a home where all are encouraged to grow to the fullness of their promise.

> First and last paragraphs by James D. Hunt
> Middle section by David H. Hunter

Sometimes both the bride and the groom have children and the marriage is a joining of two families.

Officiant: Today we celebrate not only a new relationship between Nancy and Ted, but also the beginning of new relationships between their children.

Bride: Ann and Tom, you and I have a rich life of shared memories, both good and bad. Together we have developed ways of living, habits both big and small to which we have grown accustomed. Yet all three of us have always been ready to try something new, to embark on big trips, to move to new cities, to explore new ways of living.

We are about to embark on a great adventure; the adventure of joining our family with Ted's and his two children. Jane and Peter, we are looking forward to sharing our lives with you. We know it will not always be easy, but we know that it will be an exciting adventure.

Groom: When I told Jane and Peter that we were getting married, their major problem was that it would take two months to plan the wedding. They have been looking forward to this day at least as much as I have. I know that there will be times when it will not be easy. However, I know that we are committed. We want to blend our two families into one family. We are prepared for the hard work it will take. We are ready to start out on this new adventure.

The following passage is another example of including children from previous marriages:

The officiant speaks to the child or children: You will have a share in this marriage, for your lives will inevitably be touched by the covenant into

which your mother (or your father) enters today, and your participation will be needed to develop the bonds of a new family. As this man and woman exchange their pledges in marriage, we ask from you also a pledge that you will make room in your own lives for _____.
We ask you to promise that you will join to weave a fabric of mutual help and consolation, of challenge and support. We ask that you help to create a home and a way of life in which all of you may grow into the best people you can be. In this spirit, will you recognize and honor your new relationship to _____?

The child or children respond: We will.

The officiant speaks to the bride and groom: _____ and _____, as you give yourselves to one another in love and loyalty, will you also promise always to keep room in your new life together for (children or child's name)? Will you commit yourselves to respect and honor them as individuals and members of this family? Will you pledge to cherish, encourage and tenderly care for them as long as they need you?

Bride and groom respond: We will.

Kendyl Gibbons

Lastly, in marriages in which the children are adults, they may participate by reading a selection on love and marriage. Sometimes the couple asks the children to work together on a joint statement that the oldest will read as part of the ceremony. Here is an example.

Oldest child: We wish to offer to both of you our blessing and congratulations. We love you deeply and we are delighted that you have found each other. We want you to know that just as you have always loved and supported us, we promise our love and our support for your new relationship. It is our wish for you that you live fully and deeply and that your lives together be richer and more fulfilling than either could be alone.

Chapter 11

Lighting a Unity Candle

$\mathcal{M}$ost candle lighting during a wedding service involves the lighting of a "unity candle." It can be part of a Protestant, Roman Catholic, Jewish, or contemporary service. It can be done in many ways and at any point in the service. Sometimes the couple will strike two matches (the long matches are most effective) and light a central candle. More often, two candles on either side of the unity candle are lit at the start of the wedding. At the appropriate point in the service, the couple comes forward, and each takes a lighted candle. Together they light the unity candle. Here are some examples.

The couple arrives at the front of the church or wedding hall at the beginning of the service. The officiant steps to one side, and the couple walks forward to a table. (A high table will make the candles more visible to the congregation.) As the bride and groom light the candles, the officiant speaks:

These two people come now before us to be united in marriage, just as the flames of these two candles are united into one flame.

• • •

There are five candles on a central table. All are unlit. The middle candle of the five, the unity candle, is the largest. In addition, a single lit candle is on a small table on both the left and right sides of the central table (for a total of seven candles). After the address and the readings, the officiant stands to one side. The mother and father of the groom and the mother and father of the bride come forward. Each lights one of the four candles on the central table on either side of the large central candle. They use the small lit candles on the tables on the left and right of the central table. When they finish, they hand their candles to the groom and bride who together light the central candle. The officiant says:

We witness before us today the gathering light of two families. The light from these candles symbolizes the brightness and energy created when two young people move into relationship and share their love for each other.

. . .

After the exchange of rings, the officiant steps to one side and the couple steps forward to pick up two small candles and light a large central candle. The officiant says:

May the brightness of the candle you light together shine throughout your lives, giving you courage and reassurance in the darkness. May its warmth give you shelter from the cold. And may its energy fill your spirits with strength and joy.

. . .

In the example below, the parents light two candles on either side of the unity candle. They do this at the beginning of the service after they process into the church, before they take their seats. Following the wedding vows and exchange of rings the unity candle is lit.

Officiant: In marriage, God calls a man and a woman to leave their parents to cling to one another in love, and to become one in flesh. Each of your parents has lit a candle for each of you. I now invite you to take those candles. Use them to light a candle that symbolizes your new unity, as one in the flesh, and as one in the spirit.

Michael Barlow-Sparkman

. . .

In this last example, instead of using two candles to light one candle, the couple uses one candle to light two candles. This example integrates the recognition of a child with the candle lighting ceremony by having the child also light a candle.

Officiant: _____ and _____, together you are blessed by the presence of this child, _____, who is so much a part of your family. Families grow and change through the addition of another child or the marriage of a parent to a partner. It is important for the

child to understand that this addition does not diminish the love that is available for them.

Love is like the flame of a candle. Love shines brightly throughout your home as each of you shares it.

The bride and groom each light a candle from a central candle.

Now both of your candles burn brightly, spreading light and warmth to all who stand here with you. _____ and _____, join your flames and light _____ 's candle.

The couple joins their candles making one flame, and the child lights his or her candle from that flame.

Just as you light your candles together, so may your love for each other light up your life as a family.

Laurel S. Sheridan

Chapter 12

The Huppah, the Ketubah, the Wine Cup and Yichud

*T*here are several Jewish wedding traditions that couples from all religious traditions may consider, in some form, as part of their wedding.

The Ketubah

The *Ketubah* (also spelled *Ketuba*) is a marriage contract. During a Jewish wedding, it is generally read aloud (first in Hebrew and then in English), following the giving and accepting of a ring and a declaration of consecration. Developed one thousand years ago, its inventors originally intended it to protect a woman's rights in a marriage. Signed by two witnesses, it belonged to the woman. One popular style of writing is to have two columns. One column has the Hebrew words, and the other has the English translation.

Below is the wording of the Orthodox *Ketubah*.

On the _____ [number of the day of the week of the Jewish calendar] day of the week, the _____ [number of the day of the month in the Jewish calendar] day of the month _____ _____ [name of the month in the Jewish calendar] in the year five thousand seven hundred and _____ [last two numbers in the year according to the Jewish calendar; for example 5753 is 1993 in the Christian calendar] since the creation of the world according to the reckoning which we are accustomed to use here in the city of _____ [city] in _____ [country]. That _____, son of _____ of the family _____ said to this maiden _____, daughter of _____ of the family _____, "Be my wife according to the law of Moses and Israel, and I will cherish, honor, support, and maintain you in accordance with the custom of Jewish husbands, who cherish, honor, support, and maintain their wives faithfully. And I here present you with the marriage gift of virgins, two hundred silver *zuzim*, which belongs to you, according to the law of Moses and Israel; and I will also give you your food, clothing, and necessities, and live with you as husband and wife according to the universal custom." And _____, this maiden, consented and became his wife. The trousseau that she brought to him from her father's house in silver, gold, valuables, clothing, furniture, and bed-clothes, all this _____, the bridegroom, accepted in the sum of one hundred silver pieces, and _____, the bridegroom, consented to increase this amount from his own property with the sum of one hundred silver pieces, making in all two hundred silver pieces. And thus said _____, the bridegroom, "The responsibility of this marriage contract, of this trousseau, and of this additional sum, I take upon myself and my heirs after me, so that they shall be paid from the best part of my property and possessions that I have beneath the whole heaven, that which I now possess or may hereafter acquire. All my property, real and personal, even the shirt from my back, shall be mortgaged to secure the payment of this marriage contract, of the trousseau, and of the addition made to it, during my lifetime and after my death, from the present day and forever." _____, the bridegroom, has taken upon himself the responsibility of this marriage contract, of the trousseau and the addition made to it, according to the restrictive usages of all marriage contracts and the additions to them made for the daughters of Israel, according to the institutions of our sages of blessed memory. It is not to be regarded as an indecisive contractual obligation or as a mere formula of a document. We have followed the legal formality of symbolic delivery (kinyan) between _____, son of _____, and _____, daughter of _____, this

104

maiden, and we have used a garment legally fit for the purpose, to strengthen all that is stated above,

And everything is valid
and confirmed.

Attested to _____ Witness

Attested to _____ Witness

In twentieth century America, signing the traditionally worded *Ketubah* became a formality. However, in 1973 a revised *Ketubah* appeared in the *Jewish Catalog*, and today is often used in place of the Orthodox *Ketubah*. Only the traditional wording is legal under Jewish law. However, although not legal, using a new *Ketubah* or writing your own is not forbidden by Jewish law. Below is the *Jewish Catalog Ketubah*.

On the _____ day of the week the _____ day of five thousand seven hundred _____ since the creation of the world as we reckon time here in _____.

The bride _____, daughter of _____ and _____ promised _____, the groom, son of _____ and _____. You are my husband according to the tradition of Moses and Israel. I shall cherish you and honor you as is customary among the daughters of Israel who have cherished and honored their husbands in faithfulness and in integrity.

The groom, _____, son of _____ and _____ promised _____, the bride, daughter of _____ and _____. You are my wife according to the tradition of Moses and Israel. I shall cherish you and honor you as is customary among the sons of Israel who have cherished and honored their wives in faithfulness and in integrity.

The groom and bride have also promised each other to strive through-

out their lives together to achieve an openness which will enable them to share their thoughts, their feelings, and their experiences.

To be sensitive at all times to each others' needs, to attain mutual intellectual, emotional, physical, and spiritual fulfillment. To work for the perpetuation of Judaism and of the Jewish people in their home, in their family life, and in their communal endeavors.

This marriage has been authorized also by the civil authorities of _____.

It is valid and binding.

Witness _____ Witness _____

Bride _____ Groom _____

Rabbi _____

Written by Rabbi Bernard H. Mehlman,
Rabbi Gustav Buchdahl, and
Rabbi Eugene R. Lipman

Here is a second modern *Ketubah,* written by two of the same three rabbis.

On the _____ day of the week, the _____ day of five thousand seven hundred _____ years since the creation of the world as we reckon here in the city of _____ in _____.
The bride, _____, the daughter of _____ and _____ says to the groom, "With this ring you are consecrated unto me as my husband according to the tradition of Moses and the Jewish people. I shall treasure you, nourish you, support you and respect you as Jewish women have devoted themselves to their husbands with integrity."

The groom, _____, son of _____ and _____ says to the bride, "With this ring you are consecrated unto me as my

wife according to the tradition of Moses and the Jewish people. I shall treasure you, nourish you, support you and respect you as Jewish men have devoted themselves to their wives with integrity."

We promise to be ever open to one another while cherishing each other's uniqueness to comfort and challenge each other through life's sorrow and joy; to share our intuition and insight with one another and above all to do everything within our power to permit each of us to become the persons we are yet to be.

We also pledge to establish a home open to the spiritual potential in all life. A home wherein the flow of the seasons and the passages of life are celebrated through the symbols of our Jewish heritage. A home filled with reverence for learning, loving and generosity. A home wherein ancient melody, candles and wine sanctify the table. A home joined ever more closely to the community of Israel.

This marriage has been authorized also by the civil authorities of _____.

It is valid and binding.

Witness _____ Witness _____

Bride _____ Groom _____

Rabbi _____

Written by Rabbi Bernard H. Mehlman and
Rabbi Gustav Buchdahl

Some couples prefer to write their own *Ketubah.* Here is an example.

On the _____ day of the week, the _____ day of the month _____, in the year five thousand and seven hundred and _____ since the creation of the world according to the reckoning that we are accustomed to using here in the city of _____ in _____. That _____, son of _____ of the family of _____, and _____, the daughter of _____, of the family of _____, said to each other, "Be wedded to me with this ring in keeping with the religion of the Jewish people." Each accepted the rings before witnesses, and they therefore formally united in marriage.

By these words and by the signing of this document they commit themselves to a responsible relationship. To the best of their ability they promise to respect each other's dignity. They promise to share their thoughts and experiences with honesty and candor. They promise care for each other. They promise to show concern for each other's life and growth. They promise to use their wisdom and empathy to understand each other.

Everything is valid and confirmed.

Groom _____

Bride _____

Witness _____

Witness _____

Generally the Ketubah is signed just before the wedding service. The immediate family and the rabbi gather in the rabbi's office with the witnesses. The bride and groom recite together or separately these words:

You are about to be sanctified to me as my wife/husband according to the traditions of Moses and Israel. I will love, honor, and respect you. I will provide for you and sustain you as is proper for a Jewish wife/husband to do.

The witness and (if necessary) the groom and bride sign the Ketubah. *It is given to the couple by the parents or others attending the signing.*

Rabbi: This *Ketubah*, which you now receive (from the hands of your parents), represents a heritage of family and marriage that began with our ancestors, Abraham and Sarah.

We now entrust this heritage to you. Enhance it with your commitment and devotion; bestow it upon the generations to come.

May God make you like Abraham and Sarah, who together built up the household of Israel. And let us all say: Amen.

Rabbi's Manual

The Rabbi may read the Ketubah *toward the end of the service, just before the declaration of marriage.*

The Symbolism of the Huppah

The wedding fabric that the bride and groom stand under is said to symbolize many things. For some, the fabric symbolizes the home in which the couple will live together. For others it is a symbol of clothing. The groom covers the bride with the cloth. This is symbolic of the groom taking the bride into a tent and consummating the marriage. For still others it is symbolic of Abraham's tent, which is said to have openings on all four sides so that guests coming from any direction would feel welcome.

I have officiated at several interfaith weddings where the *huppah* has been an arch covered with flowers. The arch serves as a compromise between the Jewish and Christian traditions. However, in the Jewish tradition, the *huppah* should be a fabric (not flowers) held up by four temporary wooden poles (not an arch). It is a special honor when the bride or groom invite a friend or family member to hold a pole. There are no requirements regarding the *huppah*'s size, shape or decoration. Each couple is free to use their imagination and creativity.

The Wine

A common saying in the Jewish tradition is that "without wine there is no blessing." Early in the service, after the betrothal blessings, it is custom in Jewish weddings for the bride and groom to share a glass of wine. The glass of wine is placed on a small table under the *huppah*. Lifting the cup above his or her head, the rabbi will speak, first in Hebrew and then in English. Here are several examples:

Rabbi: We praise you, Adonai our God, Ruler of the universe, Creator of the fruit of the vine.

We praise you, Adonai our God, Ruler of the universe, Creator of all things for Your glory.

We praise You, Adonai our God, Ruler of the universe, Creator of man and woman.

We praise You, Adonai our God, Ruler of the universe, who creates us as partners with You in life's everlasting renewal.

We praise You, Adonai our God, who causes Zion to rejoice in her children's happy return.

We praise You, Adonai our God, who causes bride and groom to rejoice. May these loving companions rejoice as have Your creatures since the days of creation.

Rabbi or assembly: We praise You, Adonai our God, Ruler of the universe, Creator of joy and gladness, bride and groom, love and kinship, peace and friendship. O God, may there always be heard in the cities of Israel and in the streets of Jerusalem: the sounds of joy and of happiness, the voice of the groom and the voice of the bride, the shouts of young people celebrating, the songs of children at play. We praise You, our God, who causes the bride and groom to rejoice together.

Groom and bride drink from the kiddush *cup.*

Rabbi: As you have shared the wine from a single cup, so may you, under God's guidance, share contentment, peace, and fulfillment from the cup of life. May you find life's joys heightened, its bitterness sweetened, and each of its moments hallowed by true companionship and love.

Rabbi's Manual

• • •

Rabbi: We take up this *kiddush* cup, a visible token of the heritage which endowed our people with the beauty and inner strength that make Jewish existence possible.

We pray that in many sacred moments you will partake of this cup together, making of your home a *Mikdash Me-at*, a small sanctuary.

Bride and groom: We praise You, God, Ruler of the universe, who creates the fruit of the vine.

The groom offers the cup to the bride, and the bride to the groom.

Rabbi: As you now share this wine, may you always share selflessly, ennobling and sanctifying your love.

Rabbi's Manual

• • •

Rabbi: As you share this cup of wine, you undertake to share all that the future may bring. May whatever bitterness it contains be less bitter because you share it together. May all the sweetness that it holds for you be the sweeter because you taste it together.

We praise You, Adonai our God, Ruler of the universe, Creator of the fruit of the vine.

The rabbi offers the wine to the groom and bride.

Rabbi's Manual

• • •

Officiant: Together you now drink from this cup.

As this wine comes from the earth to bring life to our bodies you will drink and live, and bring life from your living.

As this wine comes to your lips sweet and good, you drink and turn to each other sweet and good.

As the grapes of this wine have grown together sharing the earth, the sun and the rain, you shall drink and grow together to share the earth, the sun and the rain.

As this wine comes to us in peace, drink and go into the world in peace.

David A. Johnson

•   •   •

Officiant: Throughout the ages, wine has been used for celebration.

Often and among many people, wine has signified life, and a life of plenty.

Often and among many people, drinking wine from a common cup has been the mark of deep sharing.

May life bless you with happiness and plenty.

May this cup of wine be a symbol of your lifelong communion of spirit, mind, and being.

Wedding of Gordon D. Gibson and Judith L. Moore

•   •   •

The years of our lives are a cup of wine poured out for us to drink.

The grapes when they are pressed give forth their good juices for the wine.

Under the wine press of time our lives give forth their labor and honor and love.

Many days you will sit at the same table and eat and drink together.

Drink now, and may the cup of your lives be sweet and full to running over.

Kenneth L. Patton

. . .

At the end of the service, following the closing words, it is custom that a glass be broken. This can be the wine cup that was used early in the service. If the couple wishes to save this cup, another glass can be used. A light bulb wrapped in a napkin is sometimes broken instead of a wine glass because it makes an impressive "pop." However, for most people, a light bulb lacks the powerful symbolism of a glass. The officiant needs to wrap the object that is to be broken in cloth to avoid strewn broken glass.

The breaking of the glass has many symbolic meanings. According to the Talmud a father broke the first wine cup. He was upset because he felt the rabbis officiating were not sufficiently serious about the wedding service. Later, the breaking of the glass became a symbolic reminder of the destruction of the Temple in Jerusalem. More recently it has become symbolic of all the suffering of the Jewish people.

Many other explanations have been given to the act. The broken glass is a symbol of the couple breaking with the past. It is a symbol of the mixture of tragedy and joy in life. It is a symbol of the fragile nature of human relationships. It is a symbol that just as a glass cannot be repaired, a couple can never return to the way things were before their marriage.

To be inclusive of both the woman and the man, couples can use a tall wine glass, and the bride and groom together can crush it underfoot.

A Few Quiet Moments
After the Service

In the ancient past, after the Jewish service, it was custom for the groom and bride to leave the gathering, retire to their home and consummate the relationship. Although this custom was dropped centuries ago, *Yichud* (seclusion) remains a popular tradition. After the ceremony, the bride and groom retreat to a prearranged room for about fifteen minutes. Part of the tradition is for the bride and groom to feed each other a small amount of food. This is symbolic of the fact that they will support each other in their relationship.

This idea of the bride and groom spending a few moments alone together after the service goes against the American tradition of the receiving line. However, it is an idea couples should consider. It gives the bride and groom a moment to savor together the joy of their wedding, in the middle of a busy, noisy celebration.

Chapter 13

A Jewish-Christian Interfaith Service

The percentage of Jews marrying non-Jews has risen from about 6 percent in 1960 to 57 percent today. As a society we have become more permissive about marriage between people of different backgrounds. With this change, we have created a new world of human relations that we do not yet understand well.

Many rabbis fear that this relaxed attitude toward interfaith marriage among young Jews is a threat to the long-term survival of the North American Jewish community. If the number of Jews marrying non-Jews has gone from 6 percent to 57 percent, what lies ahead for the next generation? Although in one third of the couples the non-Jewish person converts to Judaism, there is still considerable reason for rabbis to fear the decline of their faith. One Jewish leader writes: "It doesn't matter to Christendom whether they lose a few followers. In the United States alone there are 142 million Christians. But there are only five and a half million Jews here, and fewer than fifty years ago Hitler did away with six million others around the world." Another Jewish leader put it this way: "If trends continue, America will become one big dull glob of people who won't even know they had a grandmother."

Orthodox and Conservative rabbis refuse to officiate at mixed marriages. Reform rabbis are divided on the issue. The Central Conference of American Rabbis has asked its members to refrain from officiating at mixed marriages. However, some Reform Rabbis do officiate at interfaith marriages, and a few will share the service with a minister or a priest.

Many Catholics and Protestants believe their religion is the one true

religion. They feel they have a duty and a responsibility to convert all the people of the earth to Christianity. Many priests refuse to participate in interfaith marriage wedding services, unless the Catholic partner signs an agreement saying that the children will be raised Catholic. Some Protestant clergy will refuse to marry persons unless they convert.

The problems interfaith couples face are not limited to hostility from organized religions. Many parents find interfaith marriage a threat to the stability of their families. In the play *Fiddler on the Roof*, Tevye says to his Jewish daughter who wants to marry a Christian: "As the Good Book says, each shall seek his own kind. Which translated means, 'A bird may love a fish, but where would they build a home together?'"

In more than one third of the interfaith marriages there is strong opposition by at least one set of parents. Rabbi Edwin Friedman, a marriage and family therapist, suggests one theory about why this is so. Friedman has counseled over two thousand interfaith couples. He believes that people who choose interfaith marriage have an especially important role in their family of origin. These children play a stabilizing role within their parents' marriage. They are like a leg in a tripod. They add stability to the family unit.

Friedman speculates that for these children, the process of maturing and extricating themselves from the snug and intense emotional ties of their families is a difficult task. He suggests that these children may select a marriage partner with a different religious or ethnic background to help them become more independent from their parents. Interfaith marriage is a way for children to break away from a family that has become too close and intense to allow the children to grow and move freely.

Friedman writes that parents may claim that they are angry about the marriage because they are concerned with the preservation of roots and tradition in their families. However, he discounts these reasons because frequently the parents are not making efforts in other parts of their lives to preserve their cultural heritage. Instead, Friedman suggests, they are angry because the marriage threatens their own emotional needs.

He advises couples who experience hostility from their parents to get distance from the emotional storm whirling around them. The couple should think about their values, writes Friedman. They need to define clearly what they want for themselves, and to develop the strength to hold to that position. He suggests that a couple in an interfaith marriage keep the

lines of communication open with their parents and other relatives. He encourages the couple to keep saying to the parents, "We love you." Over time, he says, most parents become more accepting. The marriage threatens their need to feel loved. This is the source of their anger. If you keep telling your relatives you love them, the anger may gradually decrease.

Often the most difficult crisis that interfaith couples face is how to raise their children. It has long been the position of priests, ministers and rabbis that children raised in two different faiths will grow up to be spiritually confused and unhappy adults. A book called *Mixed Blessings* by Rachel and Paul Cowan takes this position. The authors are a Jewish husband and a Unitarian wife. The wife has converted to Judaism. They write that when parents raise children in two religions or two ethnic traditions, the children grow up feeling rootless and on the fringes of two cultures. They believe children value clarity and a sense of security. According to the Cowans, children want roots in one parent's religion with branches that extend to the other parent's heritage. The book quotes a man whose Jewish father and Protestant mother raised him in a Unitarian church. He says, "I have to adapt to whomever I'm around. I wish my parents had given me a single heritage . . . I feel like I'm a chameleon."

The book *Mixed Blessings* frowns on the word "both." The authors say it is the choice parents make when they are avoiding responsibility and settling for a religious and cultural education that makes for a confused child. Using this philosophy, many ministers, priests and rabbis say to parents: "You have to choose the mother's tradition or the father's tradition. It is bad for the children if you don't decide."

In contrast, the book *Raising Your Jewish/Christian Child* presents a different view. The author, Lee Gruzen, is a Protestant woman who is married to a Jewish man. They have made the commitment to raise their children in both their Christian and Jewish heritages.

Lee Gruzen sought out and interviewed people whose parents raised them in two cultural traditions. Far from being wounded and downtrodden, she found people who were dynamic, intelligent and successful human beings. They were proud of their mixed birth and the advantages it gave them. Humor, adaptability and open-mindedness were among the many achievements of people raised in the traditions of both their parents.

Gruzen suggests that there is not one right answer about how parents

should raise children in an interfaith marriage. Each couple must decide for themselves, at their own pace. She does suggest that raising a child in both traditions is one reasonable option.

In my own experience, the way parents handle differences about religion and culture in the home teaches children how to treat people throughout their lives. A spirit of compromise, patience and sensitivity to others goes a long way toward preparing children to approach the world with openness and sensitivity. Couples who work out creative ways of negotiation about religion teach their children by example to negotiate creatively. In contrast, sometimes children see differences denied or reconciled because of one parent's domination and another's abandoning his or her identity in submission. In these situations a different model for dealing with life is taught to the child.

An Interfaith Service

This is an example of a wedding service where one person came from a Jewish background and one from a Christian background. The goal of the couple was to have a service that reflected their values and that would not offend their families. The service also suggested this couple's ability to raise any children they might have in an atmosphere of appreciation for both parent's religious inheritances.

Candle Lighting

In the Jewish tradition the lighting of candles is associated with the joy of Shabbat and the holidays. In the Christian tradition the lighting of candles to mark the beginning of a worship service is common. The officiant lights a candle and turns to the couple and congregation and speaks:

From every human being there rises a light that reaches straight to heaven. And when two souls that are destined for each other and find one another, their streams of light flow together and a single brighter light goes forth from their united being.

Baal Shem Tov[2]

---

[2]From the Rabbi Burt Jacobson, "Jewish Wedding Workbook," p. 60, quoted in *The New Jewish Wedding*, p. 103.

Opening Words

Officiant: We who gather here today are separated by the many different experiences that we have had. We have each had distinct families and friends. We have grown up in different places, and we have worked at different jobs. Some of us are male and some of us are female. We are distinct because we have different parents.

Yet we gather here today in this place because we share something in common. We share a desire to affirm and support the relationship of _____ and _____.

Marriage is an act of will, a promise to work for a communion with another person. It is not simply a spontaneous emotional reaction, nor the sudden grip of an irresistible feeling.

Marriage requires a commitment to care for another person. By caring, we show concern for the life and growth of those whom we love.

Marriage requires a commitment to take responsibility for another person. By responding we experience the needs of the other person and try to help meet those needs.

Marriage requires a commitment to respect another person. By respecting we help another person grow and unfold for their own sake. In doing so we experience the unique individuality of that person.

Marriage requires a commitment to understand another person. By understanding we transcend our own egos and see the other person in their own terms. When we use reason and humility to understand another person, we also discover ourselves.

All these commitments require that we give ourselves to another person. By giving we experience our strength, our vitality, our power. We experience ourselves as overflowing and alive.

Today we affirm and celebrate the wedding of _____ and _____.

The Question of Intent
(From the Protestant Tradition)

The officiant says to the bride:

_____, will you have this man to be your husband, to live together in the covenant of marriage? Will you love him, comfort him, honor and keep him, in sickness and in health? Forsaking all others, will you be faithful to him as long as you both shall live?

The bride answers:

I will.

The officiant says to the groom:

_____, will you have this woman to be your wife, to live together in the covenant of marriage? Will you love her, comfort her, honor and keep her, in sickness and in health? Forsaking all others, will you be faithful to her as long as you both shall live?

The groom answers:

I will.

Gift of Flowers

The officiant then addresses the congregation, saying:

These flowers, which _____ and _____ give to _____ and _____, symbolize the love that _____ and _____ have for their parents. Their new relationship has its roots in the many generations of love, respect and

hard work of their families. As they go forward into the future they shall remember and respect the traditions of each of their families.

The couples present flowers to each parent.

The Vows

Officiant: I invite you to share your vows.

Groom: _____, I love you and I promise to live with you as your husband. I shall care for you all the days of my life and share with you our experiences of joy and sadness. I promise to honor and respect the traditions and customs of your family heritage and your religious heritage as we work together to build our relationship.

Bride: _____, I love you and I promise to live with you as your wife. I shall care for you all the days of my life and share with you our experiences of joy and sadness. I promise to honor and respect the traditions and customs of your family heritage and your religious heritage as we work together to build our relationship.

The Rings

Officiant: May I have the bride's ring please?

Bless, O God, this ring, to be a sign of the vows by which this man and this woman have bound themselves to each other.

Groom: I give you this ring as a sign for all to see of the commitment of love I have made to you.

Officiant: May I have the groom's ring please?

Bless, O God, this ring, to be a sign of the vows by which this man and this woman have bound themselves to each other.

Bride: I give you this ring as a sign for all to see of the commitment of love I have made to you.

The Wine

Officiant: This bottle of wine is opened for the first time, and symbolizes the beginning of a new marriage, a new relationship.

The bride and groom pour out a small amount of wine and drink from the same cup.

Ketubah

Officiant: In the Jewish tradition a marriage contract, called a *Ketubah*, is often signed before the wedding ceremony. In keeping with this tradition, before this service _____ and _____ signed this statement, in the presence of two witnesses, their good friends, _____ and _____. They have asked me to read the statement they have signed:

You and I are in a relationship that I value and want to keep. Yet each of us is a separate person with unique needs and the right to meet those needs.

When you are having problems meeting your needs, I will try to listen with genuine acceptance, to help you find your own solutions instead of depending on mine. I also will try to respect your right to choose your own beliefs and develop your own values, different though they may be from mine.

However, when your behavior interferes with what I must do to get my own needs met, I will tell you openly and honestly how your behavior affects me, trusting that you respect my needs and feelings enough to try to change the behavior that is unacceptable to me. Also, whenever some behavior of mine is unacceptable to you, I hope you will tell me openly and honestly so I can try to change my behavior.

At those times when we find that either of us cannot change to meet the other's needs, let us acknowledge we have a conflict and commit ourselves to resolve each such conflict without either of us resorting to the use of power or authority to win at the expense of the other's losing. I respect your needs, but I also must respect my own. So let us always strive to search for a solution that will be acceptable to both of us. Your needs will be met, and so will mine—neither will lose, both will win.

In this way, you can continue to develop as a person through satisfying your needs, and so can I. Thus, ours can be a healthy relationship in which both of us can strive to become what we are capable of being, and we can continue to relate to each other with mutual respect, love and peace.

"A Credo for My Relationships,"
Thomas Gordon[3]

The Declaration

Officiant: Before these witnesses and in keeping with ancient custom, _____ and _____ have joined hands, stated their vows to each other, exchanged rings and shared wine together. Therefore I declare that they are husband and wife.

Breaking of the Glass

The officiant wraps the glass in a napkin or handkerchief and places it on the floor.

Officiant: The crushing of the glass from which the wine of celebration has been shared is a tradition of uncertain origin that suggests many

---

[3]Thomas Gordon is the founder of a program called Effectiveness Training. The program helps people learn to live the values stated in this credo. For more information write Effectiveness Training Inc. 531 Stevens Ave., Solana Beach, California 92075.

things. Some say that it is a reminder of the destruction of the temple of Jerusalem, which must not be forgotten, even in moments of joy. For others, it recalls all the imperfection and brokenness of the world. It suggests that the happiness of the bride and groom is not theirs alone, but a part of the universal answer to that brokenness. Some see the shattered glass as a symbol of a break with the past, which makes possible new relationships, or the irreplaceable and unsharable uniqueness of the marriage bond. Still another ancient blessing wishes that the years of happiness for these two people shall be no less than it would take to fit all the resulting fragments together again. So be it for _____ and _____.

Kendyl Gibbons

Together the groom and bride crush the glass with their feet.

Officiant: Congratulations! You may kiss.

•　•　•

I have touched on only a few aspects of the Jewish-Christian wedding. For more information on the subject of Jewish weddings and on the subject of interfaith marriage, consider the following:

Cowan, Paul, with Cowan, Rachel. *Mixed Blessings: Marriage between Jews and Christians.* New York: Doubleday, 1987.

Diamant, Anita. *The New Jewish Wedding.* New York: Summit Books, 1985.

Friedman, Edwin. "The Myth of the Shiksa." *Ethnicity and Family Therapy,* eds. McGoldrick, Pearce, and Giordano: pp. 499–526. New York: The Gulford Press, 1982.

Gruzen, Lee. *Raising Your Jewish Christian Child: Wise Choices for Interfaith Parents.* New York: Dodd, Mead & Company, 1987.

Mayer, Egon. *Love and Tradition: Marriage Between Jews and Christians.* New York: Schocken Books, 1985.

Chapter 14

A Roman Catholic-Protestant Service

*T*he following service is distinctive in its creative use of words and music and its blending of Catholic and Protestant elements. The shape of the service is Catholic. The eucharistic prayer is Catholic (although not approved for use officially). The music is drawn from contemporary Catholic hymns. Most of the other prayers and language are adapted from the *Book of Worship* of the United Church of Christ or the *Book of Common Prayer* of the Episcopal Church.

The service imaginatively uses the rich resources of the Christian tradition while incorporating the personal commitments and lives of the couple. It took place at the Thorndike Hilton Chapel of Chicago Theological Seminary.

Opening Words

Officiant: Dear friends,
we are gathered as the people of God
to witness the marriage of Carla Amato and Stephen Martz.
We come to share in their joy
and to ask our God to bless them.

God gives human love.
Through that love,

lovers come to know each other
with mutual care and companionship.

God gives joy.
Through that joy,
    lovers may share their new life with others,
    as God shares creation with all humankind.

    With our love and our prayers,
    we support Carla and Steve
    as they now freely give themselves
    to one another.

Book of Worship

Blessing of Water

We thank you, loving God,
for the gift of creation
with which you have entrusted us.
Before the world had shape or form,
your Spirit moved over the waters.
Out of the waters of the deep,
you formed the firmament
and brought forth the earth
to sustain new forms of life.

In the time of Noah,
you washed the earth with the waters of the flood
and your ark of salvation bore a new beginning.

In the time of Moses,
your people Israel passed through the Red Sea waters
From slavery to freedom,
and crossed the flowing Jordan
to enter the promised land.

Later, you sent Jesus
who was nurtured in the water of Mary's womb
and baptized by John in the water of the Jordan;
who became living water to a woman at the Samaritan well,
washed the feet of the disciples on the night before he died,
and from whose wounded side flowed streams of living water.

The officiant pours water into bowl.

Bless by your Holy Spirit, Loving God,
this bowl of life-giving water.
May it remind the baptized of their baptism
and all of us of the new life and new beginning
that you continually offer us in your love.

Adapted from *Book of Worship*

Song of response: "Water Psalm" by Jim Hansen © 1983 Chancel Music (a division of WORD, Inc.).

As the music is sung, the couple walk through the sanctuary holding the bowl of water and a pine branch. They dip the pine branch into the water and sprinkle fine drops of cool water on the congregation.

Opening Prayer

Officiant: Gracious God,
always faithful in your love for us,
we rejoice in your presence,
and we praise you
for the ways you have touched our lives
with a variety of loving relationships

We give thanks that we have experienced
your love and care for us
in the splendor of creation,

and through the love and care
of our families, friends, and lovers.

May our participation
in this celebration of love and commitment
give us a new joy and responsiveness
to the relationships we cherish.

Adapted from Book of Worship

And may you keep us a joyful company of your people,
so that with the faithful in every place and time,
we may praise and honor you, God Most High.

Amen.

Liturgy of the Word

Reflection

The groom reflects on the meaning of the wedding for him:

Earlier this week I had a dream that is very much in the spirit of today's
first reading. I would like to begin by sharing this very personal part of
myself, which says much about how I approach our wedding.

I am staying on or near a beach that is filled with beautiful wild horses
cavorting in sun, on surf and sand. At first there is an air of disquiet, as
if from a family arguing. Then there is a scene of absolute magical
splendor, as horses—many, many of them—dash through the water
along the shore and then enter the town. People follow them and there
is much joy, for there is to be a wedding, and it feels as if all nature is
caught up in it. I watch this, at first affected by the family argument, but
then I am caught up in the excitement and splendor. I follow everyone
in the town to the wedding site, led by wild horses. It is powerful, magical, beautiful; there is harmony, and we all follow our natures.

This dream is a personal experience of the power and magic, beauty and harmony in the world God has given humankind. The first chapter of Genesis, which tells a story of creation, is a religious and cultural expression of a similar experience.

It is a story about blessing, goodness, and, of course, new beginnings. We hear all these themes in our short selection from the chapter's end.

We hear God bless humankind, just as he earlier had blessed the birds and the fishes. We hear God, too, after she has surveyed all she has created, pronounce the world "very good."

Marriage and relationships, too, are about blessing, goodness, and, obviously, new beginnings. Or in my dream language, about power, magic, beauty, harmony. This does not mean, of course, that there will never be disharmony or ugly moments.

But it is in the mysterious, wonderful alchemy of human relationships that we often come to see the beauty and splendor of the world God has given us, and that we often experience the magical power of God's blessing, of our own holiness and goodness. Carla and I have been deeply blessed by God's goodness, and have found in our relationship much of the power and magic, beauty, harmony, and splendor of God's creation. We invite you to listen now to the way these qualities are expressed in the relationship between the people Israel and their God.

First Reading

The couple invited three friends to read the words below.

Reader one: And God said, "Let us make humankind
in our image, after our likeness.
Let them have dominion over the fish of the sea
the birds of the air, and the cattle;

129

and over all the wild animals
and all the creatures that crawl on the ground.

Reader two: God created humankind in God's image;
in the divine image God created them;
male and female God created them.
God blessed them, saying:

Reader three: "Be fertile and multiply;
fill the earth and subdue it.
Have dominion over the fish of the sea,
the birds of the air,
and all the living things that move on the earth."
God also said:
"See, I give you every seed-bearing plant
all over the earth
and every tree that has seed-bearing fruit on it
to be your food;
and to all the animals of the land,
all the birds of the air,
and all the living creatures
that crawl on the ground,
I give all the green plants for food."

Reader one: And so it happened.
God looked at everything thus made
and found it very Good.

Reader two: This is the word of our God.

Genesis 1:26–2:3

Song of response: "Spirit Blowing Through Creation" by Marty Haugen ©GIA
Publications.

Reflection

The bride reflects on the meaning of the wedding for her:

The second reading is from the fifteenth chapter of John's gospel, where Jesus likens himself to a vine and his disciples to the branches. Jesus emphasizes the connection between himself and God, whom he calls his Father, and those who follow the command to love one another. As the branches cannot exist without nourishment that comes through the vine, neither can the vine exist without essential connection to the source of all life.

Through the vine, the branches are also connected to the source of life. This gospel speaks to me of the necessity and the opportunity of connection with this Source—in whatever way it manifests itself in a person's life. Through the Source of Life comes nourishment, wholeness and consciousness. In this text, Jesus invites us into the intimacy of this relationship: "Make your home in me, as I make mine in you." What is it to make one's home in the source of life, for that source to make its home in us?

I think that marriage is one way of life that reflects this intimacy, this connection as between vine dresser, vine and branches. As Steve and I are connected to each other, we are also connected to a source that is greater than both of us. God nourishes us as we nourish each other. It is my hope that we can live out this invitation of Jesus, to make our homes in God and in each other, as God is reflected through our relationship in the world.

Second Reading

The couple invited three additional friends to read the words below.

Reader one: A reading from the gospel according to John.

I am the true vine
and my loving God is the vinedresser

Every branch in me that bears no fruit
is cut away
and every branch that does bear fruit is pruned
to make it bear even more.

Reader two: You are pruned already,
by means of the word that I have spoken to you.
Make your home in me, as I make mine in you.

Reader three: As a branch cannot bear fruit all by itself
but must remain part of the vine,
neither can you unless you remain in me,
I am the vine,

Reader one: If you remain in me
and my words remain in you,
you may ask what you will
and you shall get it.

Reader two: As God has loved me,
so I have loved you.
Remain in my love.
If you keep my commandments
you will remain in my love,
just as I have kept God's commandments
and remain in God's love.

Reader three: I have told you this
so that my own joy may be in you
and your joy may be complete.
This is my commandment:
love one another,
as I have loved you.

Reader one: This is the gospel of our God.

A Roman Catholic-Protestant Service

The Question of Intent

The officiant, speaking to Carla and Steve:

> Before God, your friends, and your families,
> I ask you to affirm your willingness
> to enter the covenant of marriage
> and to share all the joys and sorrows
> of your lives and your relationship,
> whatever the future may hold.
>
> Steve, will you have Carla to be your wife,
> and will you love her faithfully
> as long as you both shall live?
>
> *Steve says*: I will, with the help of God.

Officiant: Carla, will you have Steve to be your husband,
> and will you love him faithfully
> as long as you both shall live?
>
> *Carla says*: I will, with the help of God.

The officiant, speaking to the couple's families:

Will the families of Carla and Steve please stand in support of this couple?

Before God and all assembled,
I ask you: Will you offer your prayerful blessing
and loving support to this marriage of Carla and Steve?
If so, please respond, "We will."

The families say together: We will.

The officiant, speaking to the congregation:

And will all of you, their friends and colleagues,
now stand in support of this couple?

Will you, as the people of God
pledge your support and encouragement
to the covenant commitment
that Carla and Steve are making together?
If so, please say, "We will."

The congregation says together: We will.

Book of Worship

Blessing of the Symbols

The Eucharistic symbols are two cups and one plate.

Officiant: Carla and Steve, what will you share to symbolize your love?

Carla: I will share this ring, and this cup and one plate.

Steve: And I will share this ring, and this cup and one plate.

Officiant:
Eternal God,
who in the time of Noah
gave the rainbow as a sign of promise;
bless these rings, and these cups and plate,
that they also may be signs of promises
fulfilled in lives of faithful loving.
Amen.

Book of Worship

Exchange of Vows and Symbols

Groom:

Carla, I give myself to you
to be your husband.
I promise to love and sustain you
in the covenant of marriage
from this day forward
all the days of my life.
I give you this ring, this cup,
and this plate that we shall share
as signs of my promise and love.
And I accept your love and commitment
for the great gift you are to me.

Bride:

Steve, I give you this ring and this cup
and this plate that we shall share
as a sign of my love and faithfulness.
I give myself to be your wife.
I promise to love and sustain you
in the covenant of marriage,
from this day forward,
in good times and bad,
all the days of my life.
I want my love to be a creative and
renewing force in your life.
In taking you as my husband,
I accept one of God's greatest gifts to me.

Blessing by the Congregation

Officiant: By their promises this day,
Carla and Steve have united themselves
as wife and husband in sacred covenant.
Let us raise our right hands
and join together in blessing their union:

The congregation says together these words printed in the order of service:

The grace of Christ attend you;
the love of God surround you;
the Holy Spirit keep you
that you may grow in holy love,
find delight in each other always,
and remain faithful until your lives end.
Amen.

Adapted from *Book of Worship*

Officiant: And now, while we are standing, let us offer our prayers to God:

Prayers of the Community (or Intercessions)

Officiant: In peace, we pray to you, O God:

For the relationship of Carla and Steve, and for all couples in committed relationships: may they live together in your love, and share that love with all created things. We pray to you, O God;

Congregation: Lord, hear our prayer.

Officiant: For people of every race and nation, every tongue and faith: may we love one another and treat one another justly and peaceably. We pray to you, O God.

Congregation: Lord, hear our prayer.

Officiant: For peace in the world: may a spirit of respect grow among the nations and their leaders. We pray to you, O God.

Congregation: Lord, hear our prayer.

Officiant: For peace in the church, and among people of all faiths: may a celebration of diversity become the norm, rather than an exception. We pray to you, O God.

Congregation: Lord, hear our prayer.

Officiant: For all who minister, in the churches and outside them, especially the Claretians and the Society of Helpers: may God bless their labors and multiply their fruits. We pray to you, O God.

Congregation: Lord, hear our prayer.

Officiant: For the poor, the persecuted, the sick, and all who suffer; for refugees, prisoners, and all who are in danger: may they be relieved and protected. We pray to you, O God.

Congregation: Lord, hear our prayer.

Officiant: For all who seek new life in this country, especially the Hispanic residents of South Chicago, Pilsen, and other neighborhoods: may they be welcomed as neighbors and treated with justice. We pray to you, O God.

Congregation: Lord, hear our prayer.

Officiant: For all who live with AIDS or HIV infection: may God's peace dwell in their hearts, and God's love surround them. We pray to you, O God.

Congregation: Lord, hear our prayer.

Officiant: For all who have died, especially our friends and relatives, may they rest in that place where there is no pain or grief, but life eternal. We pray to you, O God.

Congregation: Lord, hear our prayer.

Adapted from *Book of Common Prayer*

Collect After Intercessions

Loving God,
you made humankind in your own image
and cared for us generation after generation.
We ask that you hear the prayers we have offered,
and continue to look with compassion
on the whole human family;
may we all be united in bonds of love
for one another and for the beauty of creation
with which you have entrusted us;
for it is in that love
that you are found,
Creator, Redeemer, and Sanctifier. Amen.

Exchange of Peace

At this time Carla and Steve greet all the persons at the wedding by walking through the sanctuary and hugging each person.

Liturgy of the Eucharist

Songs during preparation of the table:
"Where You Go" by Larry Connolly, Roman Catholic priest with the Congregation of Saint Paul.

Sanctus, Memorial acclamation, Amen, Lamb of God, From "Mass of Creation" by Marty Haugen.

Song at communion: "We Remember" by Marty Haugen.[4]

Officiant: The congregation is invited to come forward and receive Communion.

Closing Prayer

Loving God,
We thank you for nourishing us with your presence,
both at the table and in our sharing with one another.
Send us forth now in your love
to do the work you have given us to do;
to love and serve you in one another,
mindful that all glory and honor are yours,
Holy God, now and forever.
Amen.

Adapted from *Book of Common Prayer*

Final Blessing

May God bless us
and keep us.

May God's face shine
upon us.

And may God look upon us
with kindness
and give us that peace
which passes all understanding.
Amen.

Adapted from Numbers 6:24–26

Closing song: "Canticle of the Sun" by Marty Haugen.

---

[4]All music by Marty Haugen in this service is copyrighted by GIA Publications of Chicago, 7404 South Mason Avenue, Chicago, Illinois 60638 and was used in the service with permission.

Chapter 15

A Wedding Out-of-doors

There is often no difference between the words spoken at a wedding out-of-doors and a wedding indoors. However, it is possible in the service to refer to the fact that the wedding is being held outside. Here is an example:

Reading

Officiant:

> Sometimes our life reminds me
> of a forest in which there is a graceful clearing
> and in that opening a house,
> an orchard and garden,
> comfortable shades, and flowers
> red and yellow in the sun, a pattern
> made in the light for the light to return to.
> The forest is mostly dark, its ways
> to be made anew day after day, the dark
> richer than the light and more blessed
> provided we stay brave
> enough to keep on going in.

The Country of Marriage,
Wendell Berry

Opening Words

Officiant: We gather here today under these trees and this sky to witness and celebrate the marriage of _____ and _____. The philosopher Martin Buber has written that meaning in human life arises in three ways: in relationships between people; in relationships between people and works of art, such as painting, dancing, poetry and music; and in relationships between people and nature. We feel meaning in our relationship with others when we hold each other in a loving, gentle embrace. Singing a song with friends uplifts our spirits. Watching a sunrise over the mountains fills us with a sense of awe.

Today we have gathered in this place of natural beauty to sing and dance and be joyful, in celebration of the relationship of _____ and _____. By their commitment to marry each other they are saying yes to life. Yes, it is good to be alive, to breathe the fresh air, to feel the rays of the sun, to hold each other close. It is good to make a family together, in caring and love.

The Question of Intent

Officiant: Have you come here in the midst of these natural surroundings to affirm your commitment to each other?

Bride and groom together: We have.

The Vows

Officiant: Please share your vows with each other:

Groom: _____, I promise to live with you, to encourage and cel-

ebrate your growth and fulfillment through all the changes of our lives, and to be your faithful husband. May respect for ourselves, for each other and for the earth continue to be the cornerstone of our lives together.

Bride: _____, I promise to live with you, to encourage and celebrate your growth and fulfillment through all the changes of our lives, and to be your faithful wife. May respect for ourselves, for each other and for the earth continue to be the cornerstone of our lives together.

The Rings

Officiant: What do you give to each other as a symbol of this pledge?

Groom: I give you this ring, and I welcome you into my life as the companion of my days.

Bride: I give you this ring, and I welcome you into my life as the companion of my days.

The Blessing

Officiant: These two people have been drawn together by their love for each other. May they practice self-discipline, concentration and patience throughout their relationship, for these are essential to authentic love. May they have the courage to risk pain and disappointment; for love is a risking of what we are for what we might become. And may they learn to trust each other. Trust is the ground on which all love is built.

Closing Words

Officiant: Since _____ and _____ have pledged their love and commitment to each other before these witnesses, I declare that they are husband and wife.

The spirit of God is around us in the blue sky, the feel of the wind, the taste of the water, and the fresh smells of the earth. May this mysterious spirit enter your bodies, fill your hearts and bless your lives. Amen.

Congratulations! You may kiss!

Chapter 16

A Wedding Without Clergy

*I*n some states it is possible to become legally married without a cleric, judge or justice of the peace. Such services are common among members of the Society of Friends (Quakers).

The wedding itself is a meeting for worship, held after the manner of Friends, within which the marriage takes place. The bridal couple enter the meeting and take their places at the front of the room. In giving themselves to each other, they eliminate the custom of the bride being given away by her father. No third person pronounces them husband and wife because Friends believe that God alone can create such a union and give it significance. Neither a bridal party nor an exchange of rings is necessary to Friends' procedure although both have become customary today.

In an atmosphere of quiet and reverence during worship, the couple rises. Taking each other by the hand, they make their promises, first the groom and then the bride, using the following or similar words: "In the presence of God and these our friends, I take thee . . . to be my wife (husband), promising with Divine assistance to be unto thee a loving and faithful husband (wife) so long as we both shall live."

When the couple are seated again, the marriage certificate is brought for them to sign. Then someone who previously has been asked to do so reads the certificate aloud. This is done with dignity and care to contribute to the atmosphere of worship. The meeting then continues in silent waiting upon God while those assembled share in the worship through prayer and meditation or through spoken messages.

The person chosen to close the meeting may, if desired, first make

opportunity for the bridal party to withdraw. Those present are asked to sign the certificate as witnesses to the marriage.

From *"A Quaker Marriage,"*
published by The Philadelphia Yearly Meeting,
The Religious Society of Friends

The wording of the certificate varies, but the form goes something like this:

Be it known that

Son of _____ *and* _____

and

Daughter of _____ *and* _____

having declared their intention of marriage with each other,
were so married
with the love and support of the _____ *Friends Meeting on*
this _____ *day of the* _____ *month of the year*

_____

in a meeting for worship called for the purpose of marriage held
at _____ .
On this joyful occasion
In the presence of their families and friends
They took each other to be Husband and Wife,
Promising to be loving and faithful to one another
As long as they both shall live.

Signature of the groom _____
Signature of the bride _____
And we, being present at their marriage,
Have as witnesses set our hands on this day.

_____

All persons present as witnesses are asked to sign the certificate.

Chapter 17

Writing Your Own Service: Telling Your Story

*M*ost couples do not write their own service in the sense of sitting and writing out a completely original ceremony. Many couples who do not simply accept a standard service used by a cleric or judge look through writings such as those found in this book. They select a paragraph here and a sentence there. In this way they create their own wedding service, without writing every word.

However, you may want part of the service to be completely unique and original. You may have things you want to say that only you can express.

As an example, let's assume you want to write your own words for the ring exchange. First look at the statements about rings in this book. You can see that most ring exchanges have two parts. First is the blessing of the rings by the clergy. Second is a statement by the bride and groom said as each places a ring on their partner's finger.

Next, sit with a blank sheet of paper and write on the top, "To me the ring means . . ." Write down whatever comes to mind. Don't worry about writing complete sentences. Just put down a word or a phrase, and try not to edit as you go along.

When you begin to run out of ideas, reread the examples in this book to see if they stimulate more thoughts about what the wedding ring means to you. Call a friend or two and ask them what their associations are as they think about a wedding ring. If your parents are living, call them and ask them what their rings mean to them. Ask if they remember buying their wedding rings and how they felt when they bought them. If you have already purchased the rings for your wedding, think about that experience and try to write down the feelings you had. If you have not yet bought your rings, now may be the time to do so. Pay attention to what feelings stir inside you as you buy your rings. When you get home, write down the

words and phrases that come to mind. Try not to edit as you go along. Write down what you remember, even if it feels foolish.

Set these notes aside and take a break. Later, take a colored marking pen, go over the notes and circle words that stand out, words that you might want to use in your ring exchange.

Next, decide what you wish the officiant to say. You might start with, "This ring is a symbol of . . ." or "Bless this ring, which is given by _____ to _____ as a sign of . . ." or write a beginning of your own. Write down what the ring means to you.

Next write the words that you wish to say as you put the ring on your partner's finger. "I give you this ring as a sign of . . ." or "With this ring I . . ." or create your own beginning.

If you wish to respond when your partner puts the ring on your finger, write those words. For example, "I will wear this ring to represent . . ."

You can use this process with any of the elements that go into a wedding service. As you write, think about the person to whom you will be speaking. You might have one or two friends over to your house or apartment. Read aloud to them what you have written. How does it feel? Do the words say what you mean, or do they feel overstated? The best speeches, sermons and wedding services are statements that feel true not only when spoken loudly to a large group in a dramatic religious building and followed by organ music, but also when spoken softly to a friend across a kitchen table. Exercises like this will help you avoid the tendency to make vast generalizations or negative statements such as: "All of us know, most people are not honest in their relationships." A more modest and more positive statement would be: "In their own experience, _____ and _____, have seen that it is difficult to always be open and direct in a marriage. One goal in their relationship is to strive to be honest with each other."

Stay positive. Write about what you hope for, what you will try to do, your promises and aspirations.

Ask your future spouse or your friends to help you with your writing. Most of us are sensitive about our writing and have difficulty with criticism, but all of us can benefit from comments. You might ask your future spouse or a friend to give you support by first telling you the things they liked about what you have written. After the positive comments you are more likely to be open to hearing the ways you can improve your work.

Keep it personal. A statement about your feelings and your experiences adds color and warmth and makes your wedding service unique. Most of the wedding writings in this book talk in general terms about the power of love and relationships. You can talk about specifics. People want to hear your story. Think about the first time you met, or the first time you realized that the relationship was serious. Recall the time you agreed to get married, or about the process that led you to decide to get married. Talk about details of how things smelled, how things looked, how things felt, how things tasted, and about the sounds you heard.

For opening words you might go to the site where the wedding is being held. If you can, go there around the time of day the service will occur. Compose a statement based on the experience of your five senses. Here are two examples.

We gather this afternoon in the glow of the soft yellow light of these stained glass windows, among the familiar smells of this sanctuary. You in this congregation feel the comfort of dark wooden pews and the gold cushions where you sit. In the background we can hear the muted sounds of the city that is outside these walls. This room has witnessed more than a century of religious rituals. In this space the families and friends of _____ and _____ have held past celebrations of births and marriage and memorials to the dead. In keeping with this hallowed tradition we gather in this sacred space to celebrate the union of _____ and _____.

Today as we gather in this special place for _____ and _____, be aware of the cool air against your skin. Smell the trees, the grass and the flowers. Look at the natural colors of green against the blue sky. Hear the sounds of the birds, the sounds of the wind blowing the leaves. Before you arrived at this place you were involved in many activities. You may have been rushing to complete a project, or to get dressed, or to give a baby-sitter instructions, or to find your way here in your car. Make note of all these thoughts that are running through your head, observe that they are there. If you are able, set these thoughts aside. Breathe deeply and gently. Gradually, without forcing it, be aware of your surroundings: the breezes against your skin,

the smells, the sounds, the colors. Without forcing it, be as fully present as you can be in this place. Here. Now.

This is a meaningful place for _____ and _____. In the midst of nature they feel close to God. Therefore they have asked us to gather with them under this blue sky and amid these natural surroundings to celebrate their love for each other.

Thinking about the five senses of sight, sound, touch, taste and smell can add uniqueness and color to your vows. For example, in writing your own vows, you could say:

> _____, I love you.
> I love to look at the shape of your body.
> I love to hear the sound of your voice.
> I love the feeling of my arm around your waist.
> I love the taste of your skin against my lips.
> I love the smell of your hair as I stand close to you.
> I love you and I marry you, for richer, for poorer, for better, for worse. I will be faithful to you until death do us part.

Try it yourself, reflecting on your own experience:

> _____, I love you.
> I love to look at . . .
> I love to hear . . .
> I love the feeling of . . .
> I love the taste of . . .
> I love the smell of your . . .
> I love you and I marry you, for richer, for poorer, for better, for worse. I will be faithful to you until death do us part.

You may be thinking that you simply are not a good writer. You may worry that anything you write for your wedding will sound foolish. One satire of a contemporary vow sounded something like this:

Do you promise to love, honor, cherish, obey, admire, comprehend, stimulate, arouse, energize, invigorate, adore, revere, enliven, amuse, connect with, converse with . . .

This passage reminds me to keep my sense of humor during a wedding and not to take myself too seriously. However, it also raises an important question. How can we create a meaningful wedding service that breaks with tradition and yet is also not trendy and faddish? There are no final answers, but here are some suggestions. Avoid grand abstract statements about love, marriage, God and the universe. Even expert writers are in danger of sounding pretentious, mundane or strained when they try to sound profound. Avoid awkward words and phrases like "separatenesses," or "mutual infinite instantaneous cycles." Try to avoid fashionable expressions and words. For example, sometime in the 1970s people started talking about "prioritizing," when they meant "setting priorities." You might avoid saying in your vows, "I promise when I prioritize my life, I will always put you first."

There are three keys to writing your own wedding service. Tell the story of your relationship. Focus on your positive experiences and your hopes and promises for the future. Finally, read what you have written aloud to hear what it sounds like. In his book *The Story of Your Life: Writing a Spiritual Autobiography*, professional writer Dan Wakefield described how he asked people to write about their spiritual life. After they finished, they read aloud what they had written to a supportive group. Wakefield says,

When I started to lead these courses in spiritual autobiography, I was surprised to find that the writing done in them by "amateurs" seemed to me of better quality—that is, more entertaining, more clearly expressed, more insightful—than most of the work done in courses I have taught in the writing of fiction and journalism in universities and post graduate professional school and conferences.

The writing was clear because people were telling their own stories. Use the process of writing as an opportunity to tell the story of your relationship. You can be entertaining and insightful, and the congregation will find your story fascinating.

Chapter 18

Music, the Photographer, the Site, and the Processional

$\mathcal{B}$esides the text of your wedding ceremony, other elements greatly influence the kind of wedding service you will have.

Planning the Music

I strongly encourage you to have live music as part of your wedding service. Music calms people, relaxes them, allows them to focus and center on the event before them. It speaks to an inner spiritual center that words alone seldom can reach. Although recorded music is better than no music at all, I strongly suggest that you have live music. Unless you have an outstanding sound system, recorded music sounds tinny and inferior, especially outside. There is no good substitute for live music. In planning the music for your wedding, the Minister of Music of the church I serve, John Giles, suggests five questions for couples to consider.

First, if you are getting married in a church or synagogue, what is the policy of the music staff? Some musicians, like some clergy, will have a strict policy. They will say, "This is what I play. If you are getting married here, this is what the music will be." Others will have some flexibility. They may meet with you, play several pieces and let you choose. Still others will be open to almost anything and invite you to choose the music.

Second, what style of music do you want? New age? Rock? Classical? Folk? Spiritual? Jazz? Some clergy and musicians frown on the popular songs that couples request. "If you have a favorite 'hit tune' or a theme from

151

a motion picture, play it or sing it at the reception," says one minister. Another talks about the pastor who put his head on the desk and wept after the couple asked to have the theme from "Rocky" played after the exchange of vows. An organist told me that the sentimental pop music he played for one wedding upset him so much that after the recessional, as the guests were leaving, he played "What Kind of Fool am I" on the organ. Listen and learn from the views of the musicians and clergy. Try to ensure the text of the song and the style of the song fit with the text and the style of the rest of the wedding. Try to remain faithful to the purpose and integrity of the service. However, in the end, remember it is your wedding.

Third, what are the practical considerations? Are there both an organ and a piano in the building where you are going to hold your service? If there is, which is better? How big is the space? Alternatives to the traditional organ include trumpet, violin, cello, harpsichord, harp, guitar, flute or chamber music. Some music and some instruments are more appropriate for large spaces and some are more appropriate for small spaces. If the service is out-of-doors, what music can people hear? How much money are you willing to spend? A chamber orchestra would be good, but it will cost you several thousand dollars.

Fourth, whom do you know who is a musician? Do you have a close friend who plays the flute? Is your mother a singer? Does your brother play the piano? Often having a friend or relative perform helps make the wedding special. Also, try to match the performer to the music. Don't ask your close friend who sings in the opera to sing your favorite song written by folk singer Judy Collins. If a friend or relative does perform, ask the officiant to include in the service a brief mention of whom the performer is. Have the officiant say why the performer is important to you.

Fifth, is there a song or a piece of music that is important to you? What song was sung at your parents' wedding? Is there music that speaks to your Jewish or Christian heritage? Is there a piece of music that you and your partner consider to be "your song?" Do you have a special poem or reading that might be set to music? Consider the possibility of asking a composer to turn your favorite reading into a song. You may have a friend or relative who is a composer. If not, call the music department of your local university. They can give you names of musicians who can play at your wedding and the names of composers.

Whomever you pick to play at your wedding, remember that you can-

not know whether the music is what you want until you hear it. Ask the musician if he or she will meet with you and play the music. (The musician may charge a fee for this meeting.) If this is not possible, look for a recording of the piece the musician has recommended and listen to that recording. To hear examples of classical music played at weddings, look for a compact disc called *Music for Weddings*, produced by EMI Records Ltd., of Hayes, Middlesex, England. It contains classical European music, with mostly Christian themes. Your local library may have a copy. Be aware that some Jews find two popular classical wedding marches, Wagner's *Lohengrin* and Mendelssohn's *Midsummer Night's Dream*, in bad taste at Jewish and interfaith weddings. Wagner was openly hostile to Jews, and Mendelssohn was a Jew who converted to Christianity.

When should you have music? Most services have music as a prelude to the service, during the processional, during the recessional and as a postlude. Often there is one vocal piece during the service itself. This can come at any point before the question of intent. If you decide to have music after the exchange of vows and rings, I suggest that you keep it short. The exchange of vows and rings is the natural dramatic climax of the service. The more things you place after the exchange of vows and rings, the more you detract from the climax. Music during the service generally works best as an element helping to build toward the service's climax.

Some couples choose to have music played in the background, when they and the officiant are speaking. It is common practice in some African-American churches to have the organ playing during the minister's sermon. On the other hand, many musicians and clergy strongly prefer to keep the music and the speaking parts of the service separate.

Live music is important in setting and maintaining the mood of a service. I encourage you to include it as part of your wedding.

The Photographer

Who is in charge of a wedding? The couple who is getting married? The minister? The parents? The wedding consultant? The photographer? The right answer seems obvious: The couple who is getting married is in charge. Consequently, you need to decide when you want photos to be taken and

when you do not want photos to be taken. You may conclude that you do not want photos taken during the service. You may not want flash photos during the service. You may want only one photographer taking one photo during the exchange of rings. Make the decision well before the service and pass the word to everyone who comes to the wedding with a camera. In some weddings the couple includes a few appropriate words printed in a program that is passed out before the service.

The clicking and flashing of cameras or the movement of a photographer often disrupts weddings. I have participated in weddings in which the photographer stood directly in the line of sight between the bride and the groom as the bride walked up the aisle. The bride smiled at the photographer and the groom smiled at the photographer's back. I have participated in weddings in which the photographer walked between the minister and the bride and groom during the exchange of rings to take a close-up. I participated in weddings in which the photographer roamed back and forth behind the minister. This caused the wedding guests to focus on his meandering figure instead of focusing on the wedding service. I participated in a wedding where two photographers (one of them the bride's mother) stood about ten yards to the left of the couple. During the exchange of vows they had a whispering conversation in full view and hearing of the congregation.

It is nice to have pictures. However, do your best not to let your photographer disrupt your wedding. Most photographers will respect your wishes if you make them clear ahead of time. Remember that this is your wedding, you are in charge, you are the directors, you make the decisions. When the photographer gets married, he or she can be in charge, but during your wedding you are in charge.

There are differing opinions on whether it is best to have a friend take the photos or hire a professional. My own view is, if you have the money, hire a professional photographer. The more businesslike the relationship is, the better. Interview the photographer ahead of time. Have a written contract, clearly stating what you want, how much you will pay and what happens if you find the photographs unacceptable. Here are some questions to consider:

When should photos be taken?

Where should the photographer stand?

Will the photographer move around the room during the service?

Should a flash be used?

Should there be close-ups during the service?

If you feel worried about what the photographer might do, trust that feeling. Write out what you want and don't want and add it to the contract. Often, about two minutes before the service is about to take place, the photographer comes to me and asks, "Do you mind if I take pictures during the service?" This question tempts me to say, "Yes, I do mind. I forbid you to take any photos during the service." However, the answer I do give is this: "When the photographs are taken is up to the bride and groom. Have you talked to them about this? Have they told you when they want pictures during the service? This is their decision." Make the decision about photographs long before the service begins and communicate it clearly to the photographers and the cleric.

The Site: Where to Have a Wedding

These are the choices:

A church or synagogue: This is the right choice most of the time. People create religious spaces intentionally for moments like these. Most churches and temples do not charge high fees to rent their buildings for weddings. If you are a member of a church or temple, there is often no charge for a wedding service. Religious buildings are often the most beautiful place for a wedding, and the least costly.

A hotel or banquet hall, dinner club, restaurant: These places offer package deals that might include hotel rooms for out-of-town guests, a sit-down dinner after the service, an open bar, and a hall in which to perform the wedding service. The major reason for using one of these sites is that everything takes place in the same building. Some big city hotels have their own wedding consultant as part of the package. I have experienced some unforeseen difficulties when officiating at weddings in hotels. Once, a hotel began to play background music over the loudspeakers during the ceremony. Another time the ceremony took place in a room where the kitchen was on

the other side of the wall. In the middle of the service a person in the kitchen dropped a load of dishes. The wedding guests heard not only the sound of breaking glass but also the loud cursing of the dishwasher. Yet another time I had spoken the first few words of the service when a woman's voice came over a loudspeaker: "The person with the blue Oldsmobile, license number KTC-371, must move his car immediately from the entrance or the car will be towed. I repeat: The person with the blue Oldsmobile, license number KTC-371, must move his car immediately from the front entrance or the car will be towed. You must move your car right now or we will move it for you!" I started the service again. If you decide to have a wedding at a banquet hall or hotel, look over the site carefully.

In a home: For small weddings this can be a meaningful and intimate choice. Remember to unplug the phone during the service.

Out-of-doors: The location is everything with an outdoor wedding. Such weddings tend to work better in areas of spectacular, dramatic natural beauty. In the Chicago area there are few good sites for an outdoor wedding. It is difficult to avoid the sound of cars and airplanes. On the other hand, I have officiated at many out-of-doors weddings on the coast of California, on the coast of Massachusetts and on Kentucky horse farms. Out-of-doors can be a wonderful place to have a wedding. However, pick your site carefully. Here are some things to think about:

Do you have an alternative plan in case of rain?

What about background car and airplane noise?

What about mosquitoes or bees or other insects?

Will people stand and if so, is the service short?

What will be the first thing that will happen after the service? In an indoor wedding you recess out—in an outdoor wedding there may be no place to which to recess. In this situation, one solution is to have the officiant say, "I invite you to come forward and congratulate the bride and groom."

A word about rice. Rice is a symbol of fertility, a traditional way for the guests to express their hope that the couple be successful in having children. It is not appropriate for people to throw rice inside a building. All rice

should be thrown outside. Some landscape people ban the throwing of rice outside buildings after weddings because they fear it will germinate and grow rice in their lawns or flower beds. Once a bride and groom told me I should discourage the throwing of white rice because the birds eat it, it swells inside them and kills them. They suggested birdseed instead of rice. I had visions of dead birds on their backs, feet up, lying on the walk outside the church a few hours after a wedding. Half-eaten wedding rice would be dripping from their beaks. To confirm this, I called an ornithologist at the Field Museum of Natural History in Chicago. He said he knew of no study on birds and wedding rice. However, because the bird's digestive system is so fast, he thought it unlikely that white rice would cause problems.

Other sites include sailboats, old mansions, airplane flights and so on. Ministers often have stories about their strangest weddings. I have fond memories of officiating at a wedding in San Francisco Bay on a sailboat that had been originally built for Humphrey Bogart. My strangest wedding was between two wrestlers in the ring before a match. Ten thousand people watched and booed. (The couple I married played the roles of bad guy and bad gal wrestlers in the make-believe drama of American professional wrestling.)

A Formal Christian Processional

All the references I will make to left and right are based on the perspective of a person facing the front of the room, looking toward where the service will be held.

Before the processional:

An usher escorts and seats the groom's mother on the right side facing the front. They walk down the aisle, the usher on the right and the mother of the groom on the left. The father of the groom follows the usher and the mother of the groom. The front row on the right side is for the groom's parents.

An usher escorts and seats the bride's mother on the left side facing the

front. They walk down the aisle, the usher on the right and the mother of the bride on the left. The front row on the left side is for the bride's parents.

The white runner or carpet for the aisle is unrolled by two ushers.

The processional starts.

The officiant enters from a side entrance or comes up a side aisle from the back, if there is no side entrance. The officiant takes his or her position. This is often the signal for the musicians to complete the prelude music and begin the processional music.

The groom and best man follow the officiant and enter from the side entrance or from a side aisle. They should take their position on what is the right side of the room when you are facing toward the front of the room. After arriving, the best man and the groom should turn and look down the center aisle and watch the procession.

If you wish, after the groom and best man are in place, the mother of the bride may stand and turn to watch the procession. The rest of the congregation should then stand, also turning to watch the procession, following the lead of the mother of the bride. In real life this does not always happen, leaving the mother of the bride standing alone, or with her husband and a few others. To make sure everyone stands, have a written order of service stating clearly when you want people to stand.

The ushers process in, often two at a time. Often the ushers are male friends of the groom and stand in a line on the outside of the best man.

The bridesmaids follow most often one at a time, sometimes in pairs. They are often female friends of the bride and stand in a line on the outside of where the bride will stand.

The maid or matron of honor follows.

The ring bearer follows the maid or matron of honor. Often there is no ring bearer. Then the best man takes charge of the rings, or the best man and maid or matron of honor share the responsibility.

The children tossing out flower petals follow. Although we traditionally think of one flower girl, I have often seen two children, a girl and a boy, sharing this role.

The musician increases the volume of the music. This is another point in the service where the mother of the bride might stand (if she is not already

standing) and turn to watch the entrance of her daughter. The rest of the congregation should follow her example and also stand and turn to watch the bride's entrance. To insure that they stand have it in writing in an order of service.

The bride enters on her father's right arm. At the altar the bride joins the groom, and her father takes his seat by his wife.

The Recessional

The musician starts to play the recessional music.

The bride and groom walk down the center aisle with the bride on the left facing the front, groom on the right.

The flower bearers and ring bearer may follow, but most often they seek out and join their parents.

Most often the men and women standing on either side pair off and recess together. The best man and the maid or matron of honor goes first. The usher who was next to the best man and the bridesmaid who was next to the maid of honor goes next, and so on.

Next, the bride's mother and father often depart together after the last usher and bridesmaid.

The groom's mother and father often depart together after the bride's mother and father.

Last, the congregation walks to the back to greet the wedding party.

Jewish Tradition

A major difference in the processional is that often the groom is brought to the *huppah* by his parents and the bride is brought to the *huppah* by her parents. This symbolically represents the uniting of two families. This is based in tradition. No Jewish laws or rules require a particular processional or recessional order.

Often in Jewish weddings the bride's parents or family and the groom's parents or family stand on the appropriate sides. They stand to the back of the wedding party during the entire service, after they have escorted the

bride and groom to the *huppah*. This dictates a big staging area, but can be moving in its symbolism.

When standing under the *huppah*, the positions of the bride and groom are the reverse of a Christian wedding. The groom should take his position on what is the left side of the room when people are facing forward toward the front of the room. The bride should stand on the right. Often in Jewish weddings the entire congregation follows this practice. The groom's friends and family are on the left side, and the bride's friends and family are on the right side. In a Jewish Orthodox wedding women and men sit on separate sides of the room. These are customs. No Jewish laws instruct people to stand or sit in a particular place.

Alternatives to Traditional Processionals and Recessionals

It is your wedding. You have the right to organize the entrance and exit in any way that feels best to you. For example, the bride and groom can walk in together. In some rooms, or out-of-doors, you can arrange chairs in a circle, and the bride and groom can sit in the circle, standing when the service begins. In smaller, less formal weddings, you can do away with the recessional. Simply have the officiant say at the end of the service, "I now invite the congregation to leave their seats and come forward and greet _____ and _____."

If you are feeling anxious about this part of the service, or if many people are involved, have a rehearsal. Practice both your entrance and your exit twice. In my experience, the first time we run through the processional and recessional there is often a great deal of joking and confusion. Generally, by the time we have walked through it twice, people have settled down and know their parts.

Should every wedding have a rehearsal? Have a rehearsal when you have planned a complicated wedding, involving many people. Have a rehearsal when your service has many parts such as a reading by a friend, unity candles, gifts of flowers, and a song. Have a rehearsal when you are

feeling anxious about the service. The rehearsal should calm you so you can better enjoy the actual wedding. However, if you have a simple service and you feel relaxed, you may not need a rehearsal.

If during the wedding, someone stands in the wrong place or enters or leaves in the wrong order, don't fret about it. You are there to celebrate your relationship. This celebration will happen, even when the details of walking in and out don't go as planned.

The details are not important. The spirit of commitment you each bring to your relationship is important. Secure in this commitment, you can relax and enjoy your wedding.

Appendices

A Book of Common Prayer Ceremony

The Celebration and Blessing
of a Marriage

Opening Words

At the time appointed, the persons to be married, with their witnesses, assemble in the church or some other appropriate place.

During their entrance, a hymn, psalm or anthem may be sung or instrumental music may be played.

Then the celebrant, facing the people and the persons to be married, with the woman to the right and the groom to the left, addresses the congregation and says:

Dearly beloved: We have come together in the presence of God to witness and bless the joining together of this man and this woman in Holy Matrimony. The bond and covenant of marriage was established by God in creation, and our Lord Jesus Christ adorned this manner of life by his presence and first miracle at a wedding in Cana of Galilee. It signifies to us the mystery of the union between Christ and his Church, and Holy Scripture commends it to be honored among all people.

The union of husband and wife in heart, body, and mind is intended by God for their mutual joy; for the help and comfort given one another in prosperity and adversity; and, when it is God's will, for the procreation of children and their nurture in the knowledge and love of the Lord. Therefore marriage is not to be entered into unadvisedly or lightly, but

reverently, deliberately, and in accordance with the purposes for which it was instituted by God.

In the opening exhortation, the full names of the persons to be married are declared. Subsequently, only their first names are used.

Into this holy union _____ and _____ now come to be joined. If any of you can show just cause why they may not lawfully be married, speak now; or else forever hold your peace.

Then the celebrant says to the persons to be married:

I require and charge you both, here in the presence of God, that if either of you know any reason why you may not be united in marriage lawfully, and in accordance with God's Word, you do now confess it.

The Question of Intent

The celebrant says to the bride:

_____, will you have this man to be your husband; to live together in the covenant of marriage? Will you love him, comfort him, honor and keep him, in sickness and in health; and, forsaking all others, be faithful to him as long as you both shall live?

The bride answers:

I will.

The celebrant says to the groom:

_____, will you have this woman to be your wife; to live together in the covenant of marriage? Will you love her, comfort her, honor and keep her, in sickness and in health; and, forsaking all others, be faithful to her as long as you both shall live?

The groom answers:

I will.

The celebrant then addresses the congregation, saying:

Will all of you witnessing these promises do all in your power to uphold these two persons in their marriage?

People: We will.

If there is to be a presentation or a giving in marriage, it takes place at this time.

A hymn, psalm or anthem may follow.

The celebrant then says to the people:

The Lord be with you.

People: And also with you.

Let us pray.

O gracious and ever living God, you have created us male and female in your image. Look mercifully upon this man and this woman who come to you seeking your blessing, and assist them with your grace, that with true fidelity and steadfast love they may honor and keep the promises and vows they make; through Jesus Christ our Savior, who lives and reigns with you in the unity of the Holy Spirit, one God, for ever and ever. Amen.

The Readings

Then one or more of the following passages from Holy Scripture is read. If there is to be a Communion, a passage from the Gospel always concludes the Readings.

Old Testament, Genesis 1:26–28 (Male and female he created them)
Genesis 2:4–9, 15–24 (A man cleaves to his wife and they become one flesh)
Song of Solomon 2:10–13, 8:6–7 (Many waters cannot quench love)
Tobit 8:5b–8 (New English Bible) (That she and I may grow old together)

New Testament, I Corinthians 13:1–13 (Love is patient and kind)
Ephesians 3:14–19 (The Father from whom every family is named)
Ephesians 5:1–2, 21–33 (Walk in love, as Christ loved us)
Colossians 3:12–17 (Love which binds everything together in harmony)
I John 4:7–16 (Let us love one another for love is of God)

Between the Readings, a psalm, hymn, or anthem may be sung or said. Appropriate psalms are 67, 127 and 128.

When a passage from the Gospel is to be read, all stand, and the Deacon or Minister appointed says:

The Holy Gospel of our Lord Jesus Christ according to _____.

People: Glory to you, Lord Christ.

New Testament, Matthew 5:1–10 (The Beatitudes)
Matthew 5:13–16 (You are the light . . . let your light so shine)
Matthew 7:21, 24–29 (Like a wise man who built his house upon the rock)
Mark 10:6–9, 13–16 (They are no longer two but one)
John 15:9–12 (Love one another as I have loved you)

After the Gospel, the reader says:

The Gospel of the Lord.

People: Praise to you, Lord Christ.

A homily or other response to the Readings may follow.

A Book of Common Prayer Ceremony

The Vows

The groom, facing the bride and taking her right hand in his, says:

In the Name of God, I, _____, take you, _____, to be
my wife, to have and to hold from this day forward, for better for
worse, for richer for poorer, in sickness and in health, to love and to
cherish, until we are parted by death. This is my solemn vow.

*Then they loose their hands, and the bride, still facing the groom, takes his right
hand in hers, and says:*

In the Name of God, I, _____, take you, _____, to be
my husband, to have and to hold from this day forward, for better for
worse, for richer for poorer, in sickness and in health, to love and to
cherish, until we are parted by death. This is my solemn vow.

They loose their hands.

The Rings

The celebrant may ask God's blessing on a ring or rings as follows:

Bless, O Lord, this ring to be a sign of the vows by which this man and
this woman have bound themselves to each other; through Jesus Christ
our Lord. Amen.

The giver places the ring on the ring finger of the other's hand and says:

_____, I give you this ring as a symbol of my vow, and with all
that I am, and all that I have, I honor you, in the Name of the Father,
and of the Son, and of the Holy Spirit (or in the Name of God).

Then the celebrant joins the right hands of husband and wife and says:

Now that _____ and _____ have given themselves to

each other by solemn vows, with the joining of hands and the giving and receiving of a ring, I pronounce that they are husband and wife, in the Name of the Father, and of the Son, and of the Holy Spirit.

Those whom God has joined together let no one put asunder.

People: Amen.

The Blessing

All standing, the celebrant says:

Let us pray together in the words our Savior taught us.

People and celebrant:

> Our Father in heaven,
>   hallowed be your Name,
>   your kingdom come,
>   your will be done,
>   on earth as in heaven.
>   Give us today our daily bread.
>
> Forgive us our sins
>   as we forgive those
>   who sin against us.
>   Save us from the time of trial,
>   and deliver us from evil.
>   For the kingdom, the power,
>   and the glory are yours,
>   now and for ever. *Amen.*

If Communion is to follow, the Lord's Prayer may be omitted here.

The deacon or other person appointed reads the following prayers, to which the people respond, saying, "Amen."

If there is not to be a Communion, one or more of the prayers may be omitted.

Let us pray.

Eternal God, creator and preserver of all life, author of salvation, and giver of all grace: Look with favor upon the world you have made, and for which your Son gave his life, and especially upon this man and this woman whom you make one flesh in Holy Matrimony. Amen.

Give them wisdom and devotion in the ordering of their common life, that each may be to the other a strength in need, a counselor in perplexity, a comfort in sorrow, and a companion in joy. Amen.

Grant that their wills may be so knit together in your will, and their spirits in your Spirit, that they may grow in love and peace with you and one another all the days of their life. Amen.

Give them grace, when they hurt each other, to recognize and acknowledge their fault, and to seek each other's forgiveness and yours. *Amen.*

Make their life together a sign of Christ's love to this sinful and broken world, that unity may overcome estrangement, forgiveness heal guilt, and joy conquer despair. Amen.

Bestow on them, if it is your will, the gift and heritage of children, and the grace to bring them up to know you, to love you, and to serve you. Amen.

Give them such fulfillment of their mutual affection that they may reach out in love and concern for others. Amen.

Grant that all married persons who have witnessed these vows may find their lives strengthened and their loyalties confirmed. Amen.

Grant that the bonds of our common humanity, by which all your children are united one to another, and the living to the dead, may be so

171

transformed by your grace, that your will may be done on earth as it is in heaven; where, O Father, with your Son and the Holy Spirit, you live and reign in perfect unity, now and forever. Amen.

The people remain standing. The husband and wife kneel, and the celebrant says one of the following prayers:

Most gracious God, we give you thanks for your tender love in sending Jesus Christ to come among us, to be born of a human mother, and to make the way of the cross to be the way of life. We thank you, also, for consecrating the union of man and woman in his Name. By the power of your Holy Spirit, pour out the abundance of your blessing upon this man and this woman. Defend them from every enemy. Lead them into all peace. Let their love for each other be a seal upon their hearts, a mantle about their shoulders, and a crown upon their foreheads. Bless them in their work and in their companionship; in their sleeping and in their waking; in their joys and in their sorrows; in their life and in their death. Finally, in your mercy, bring them to that table where your saints feast for ever in your heavenly home; through Jesus Christ our Lord, who with you and the Holy Spirit lives and reigns, one God, for ever and ever. Amen.

or this:

O God, you have so consecrated the covenant of marriage that in it is represented the spiritual unity between Christ and his Church: Send therefore your blessing upon these your servants, that they may so love, honor, and cherish each other in faithfulness and patience, in wisdom and true godliness, that their home may be a haven of blessing and peace; through Jesus Christ our Lord, who lives and reigns with you and the Holy Spirit, one God, now and for ever. Amen.

Closing Words

The husband and wife still kneeling, the celebrant adds this blessing:

God the Father, God the Son, God the Holy Spirit, bless, preserve, and keep you; the Lord mercifully with his favor look upon you, and fill you with all spiritual benediction and grace; that you may faithfully live together in this life, and in the age to come have life everlasting. Amen.

The celebrant may say to the people:

The peace of the Lord be always with you.

People: And also with you.

    The newly married couple then greet each other, after which greetings may be exchanged throughout the congregation.
    When Communion is not to follow, the wedding party leaves the church. A hymn, psalm or anthem may be sung, or instrumental music may be played.

A Roman Catholic Ceremony

$\mathcal{T}$he text that follows is merely a sample of the variety of prayers and readings that the *Rite of Marriage* provides. In almost every case there are options besides these. A Catholic couple is free to choose any of the texts. Reverend Monsignor Alan F. Detscher, Associate Director, Secretariat for the Liturgy of the National Conference of Catholic Bishops writes:

> Catholics are not free to use prayers from other rites during the marriage ceremony. If a Catholic marries a Protestant or Jew and the bishop has given the required permission, the marriage may take place before a minister or rabbi and the rite of a Protestant or Jewish partner may be used. In such a case a Catholic priest might attend and participate, but he would not receive the vows.

The text is one example of the *Rite for Marriage* during Mass. I have chosen to show the service in the context of a Mass although many readers of this book are from mixed faiths, and therefore will not celebrate their marriage during Mass. My hope is that including the Mass will educate non-Catholics about the theology and liturgy of a Roman Catholic marriage rite.

Peter Finn, Associate Executive Secretary, the International Commission on English in the Liturgy, has written:

> If a Catholic is marrying a non-Catholic Christian, usually the rite is celebrated outside the context of a Mass. In this case a liturgy of the word precedes the actual exchange of vows. There are a number of instances now in the United States (because of the unavailability of a priest) when the rite outside Mass is used for marriages in which both spouses are Catholic. In this case a deacon may preside, or in some cases, as the new

rite provides, a layperson. Frequently Catholic spouses will choose not to have a Mass if they know that many in the community are non-Catholics and would therefore be unable to receive Communion.

Roman Catholic teaching places importance on the wedding as a commitment to the larger community. One commentator put it this way:

The liturgical celebration should manifest the fact that the spouses are undertaking a special vocation in the Christian community. It is not a personal or private affair in which the bride and groom express their love by means of gestures or words which have special significance only to them or to a select few.

At the appointed time, the priest, vested for Mass, goes to the door of the church or, if more suitable, to the alter. There he greets the bride and groom in a friendly manner, showing that the Church shares their joy.

The Opening Prayer

Words in parentheses are optional.

Almighty God,
hear our prayers for _____ and _____,
who have come here today
to be united in the sacrament of marriage.
Increase their faith in you and in each other,
and through them bless your Church (with Christian children).

We ask you this
through our Lord Jesus Christ, your Son,
who lives and reigns with you and the Holy Spirit,
one God, for ever and ever.

There may be three readings, the first of them from the Old Testament.

First Reading

A reading from the Song of Songs.

For love is as strong as death.

I hear my Beloved. See how he comes
leaping on the mountains,
bounding over the hills.
My Beloved is like a gazelle,
like a young stag.

See where he stands behind our wall.
He looks in at the window,
he peers through the lattice.

My Beloved lifts up his voice, he says to me,
"Come then, my love,
my lovely one, come.

"My dove, hiding in the clefts of the rock,
in the coverts of the cliff,
show me your face,
let me hear your voice;
for your voice is sweet
and your face is beautiful."

My Beloved is mine and I am his.
He said to me:
Set me like a seal on your heart,
like a seal on your arm.
For love is strong as Death,
jealousy relentless as Sheol.
The flash of it is a flash of fire,
a flame of the Lord himself.

Love no flood can quench,
no torrents drown.

This is the Word of the Lord.

The Jerusalem Bible, Song of Songs 2:8–10,14,16a; 8:6–7a

Second Reading

A reading from the first letter of John.

God is love.

My dear people,
let us love one another
since love comes from God
and everyone who loves is begotten by God and knows God.
Anyone who fails to love can never have known God,
because God is love.
God's love for us was revealed
when God sent into the world his only Son
so that we could have life through him;
this is the love I mean:
not our love for God,
but God's love for us when he sent his Son
to be the sacrifice that takes our sins away.
My dear people,
since God has loved us so much,
we too should love one another.
No one has ever seen God;
but as long as we love one another
God will live in us
and his love will be complete in us.

This is the Word of the Lord.

The Jerusalem Bible, 1 John 4:7–12

Third Reading

A reading from the gospel according to Matthew.

Rejoice and be glad, for your reward will be great in heaven.

Seeing the crowds, he went up the hill. There he
sat down and was joined by his disciples. Then he
began to speak. This is what he taught them:

"How happy are the poor in spirit;
theirs is the kingdom of heaven.
Happy the gentle:
they shall have the earth for their heritage.
Happy those who mourn:
they shall be comforted.
Happy those who hunger and thirst for what is right:
they shall be satisfied.
Happy the merciful:
they shall have mercy shown them.
Happy the pure in heart:
they shall see God.
Happy the peacemakers:
they shall be called sons of God.
Happy those who are persecuted in the cause of right:
theirs is the kingdom of heaven.

"Happy are you when people abuse you
and persecute you and speak all kinds of
calumny against you on my account.
Rejoice and be glad, for your reward will
be great in heaven."

This is the Gospel of the Lord.

The Jerusalem Bible, Matthew 5:1–12

The priest always follows the Gospel with a homily on the readings and the meaning of Christian marriage. He speaks about the mystery of Christian marriage, the dignity of wedded love, the grace of the sacrament. He describes the responsibilities of married people, keeping in mind the circumstances of this marriage.

The Question of Intent

All stand, including the bride and bridegroom, and the priest addresses them in these or similar words:

> My dear friends, you have come together in this church so that the Lord may seal and strengthen your love in the presence of the Church's minister and this community. Christ abundantly blesses this love. He has already consecrated you in baptism and now he enriches and strengthens you by a special sacrament so that you may assume the duties of marriage in mutual and lasting fidelity. And so, in the presence of the Church, I ask you to state your intentions.

Statement of Intentions

The priest then questions them about their freedom of choice, faithfullness to each other, and the acceptance and upbringing of children:

> _____ and _____ have you come here freely and without reservation to give yourselves to each other in marriage?

> Will you love and honor each other as man and wife for the rest of your lives?

The following question may be omitted if, for example, the couple is advanced in years.

Will you accept children lovingly from God, and bring them up according to the law of Christ and his Church?

Each answers the questions separately. The priest then invites them to declare their consent.

The Vows

The celebrant then invites them to declare their consent.

Since it is your intention to enter into marriage, join your right hands, and declare your consent before God and his Church.

They join hands. The bridegroom says:

I, _____, take you, _____, to be my wife. I promise to be true to you in good times and in bad, in sickness and in health. I will love you and honor you all the days of my life.

The bride says:

I, _____, take you, _____, to be my husband. I promise to be true to you in good times and in bad, in sickness and in health. I will love you and honor you all the days of my life.

Receiving their consent, the celebrant says:

You have declared your consent before the Church. May the Lord in his goodness strengthen your consent and fill you both with his blessings.

What God has joined, men must not divide.

Response: Amen.

The Rings

Lord,
bless these rings which we bless in your name.
Grant that those who wear them
may always have a deep faith in each other.
May they do your will
and always live together
in peace, good will, and love.

(We ask this) through Christ our Lord.

Response: Amen.

The bridegroom places his wife's ring on her ring finger. He may say:

_____, take this ring as a sign of my love and fidelity. In the name of the Father, and of the Son, and of the Holy Spirit.

The bride places her husband's ring on his ring finger. She may say:

_____, take this ring as a sign of my love and fidelity. In the name of the Father, and of the Son, and of the Holy Spirit.

General Intercessions

The intercessions begin with an invitation. The priest faces the bride and groom, and with hands joined, says:

We have listened to the word of God.
Let us now ask God to listen to us,
to bless our words of prayer
which we offer
for the people of the world.

There follows a series of intentions for the couple to which the people respond, usually saying "Lord hear our prayer."

Reader:

For leaders of Church and State
for heads of institutions
for heads of homes and households . . .
that they will lead us and guide us
in the search for God and the good life
in the search for peace and joy
in the search for love among us—
let us pray to the Lord.

People: Lord, hear our prayer.

For all married people:
for those who married yesterday
for the new couple, _____ and _____, married today for
those who will marry tomorrow . . .
that they may savor the joy of being together
warm love and children
a long life, (wine) and friends
and a new day, every day—
let us pray to the Lord.

People: Lord, hear our prayer.

For all young and single people
who look forward to a vocation
full of life and full of love—
let us pray to the Lord.

People: Lord, hear our prayer.

For the lonely old and the lonely young
for the hungry rich man
and the hungry poor man
for the sick in body, mind, and spirit

for the weak man in all of us—
let us pray to the Lord.

People: Lord, hear our prayer.

For our relatives and friends
who walk with us on life's journey
and for those who have gone before us
to the other side of life.
For the fulfillment of all their unfulfilled desires—
let us pray to the Lord.

People: Lord, hear our prayer.

Priest:
These are words of prayer today
for ourselves and all human beings.
Tomorrow there will be others.
Lord God the beloved of humankind
who has first loved us
give our words by your listening
the power of your word
so that all things may be accomplished
sweetly and gently
for the happiness of all.
Through Christ our Lord.

People: Amen.

The Eucharist

*If the assembly is to celebrate the Eucharist within the wedding liturgy, the service
will include a "prayer over the gifts" (the gifts are the bread and wine), introductory
dialogue and a preface that begins the Eucharistic prayer. Catholics do not practice*

intercommunion and so it is usually not appropriate for a marriage of a Catholic and a non Catholic to take place during Mass. Therefore, if the marriage is between a Catholic and a Protestant or a Jew, the assembly would not celebrate the Eucharist. In this case the priest would omit the Prayer over the Gifts, preface, and prayer after Communion.

Prayer Over the Gifts

Lord,
accept our offering
for this newly married couple, _____ and _____.
By your love and providence you have brought
them together;
now bless them all the days of their married life.

(We ask this) through Christ our Lord.

Preface: Introductory Dialogue

Priest: The Lord be with you.
People: And also with you.

Priest: Lift up your hearts.
People: We lift them up to the Lord.

Priest: Let us give thanks to the Lord our God.
People: It is right to give him thanks and praise.

Preface

Father, all-powerful and ever-living God,
we do well always and everywhere to give you thanks.

By this sacrament your grace unites man and woman
in an unbreakable bond of love and peace.

You have designed the chaste love of husband and
wife
for the increase both of the human family
and of your own family born in baptism.

You are the loving Father of the world of nature;
you are the loving Father of the new creation of
grace.
In Christian marriage you bring together the two
orders of creation:
nature's gift of children enriches the world
and your grace enriches also your Church.

Through Christ the choirs of angels
and all the saints
praise and worship your glory.
May our voices blend with theirs
as we join in their unending hymn:

Holy, holy, holy Lord, God of power and might,
heaven and earth are full of your glory.
Hosanna in the highest.
Blessed is he who comes in the name of the Lord.
Hosanna in the highest.

The Nuptial Blessing

The priest faces the bride and groom and, with hands joined, says:

My dear friends, let us turn to the Lord and pray
that he will bless with his grace this woman (or _____.)
now married in Christ to this man (or _____.)
and that (through the sacrament of the body and blood of Christ,)
he will unite in love the couple he has joined in this holy bond.

All pray silently for a short while. Then the priest extends his hands and continues:

Father, by your power you have made everything out of nothing.
In the beginning you created the universe
and made mankind in your own likeness.

You gave man the constant help of woman
so that man and woman should no longer be two, but one flesh,
and you teach us that what you have united
may never be divided.
Father, you have made the union of man and wife so holy a mystery
that it symbolizes the marriage of Christ and his Church.
Father, by your plan man and woman are united,
and married life has been established
as the one blessing that was not forfeited by original sin
or washed away in the flood.
Look with love upon this woman, your daughter,
now joined to her husband in marriage.
She asks your blessing.
Give her the grace of love and peace.
May she always follow the example of the holy women
whose praises are sung in the scriptures.
May her husband put his trust in her
and recognize that she is his equal
and the heir with him to the life of grace.
May he always honor her and have her
as Christ loves his bride, the Church.
Father, keep them always true to your commandments.
Keep them faithful in marriage
and let them be living examples of Christian life.
Give them the strength which comes from the gospel
so that they may be witnesses of Christ to others.
(Bless them with children
and help them to be good parents.
May they live to see their children's children.)

And, after a happy old age,
grant them fullness of life with the saints
in the kingdom of heaven.
(We ask this) through Christ our Lord. Amen.

If the marriage takes place within the context of a Mass, the assembly exchanges the sign of peace. The sign of peace often takes the form of shaking hands or hugging the person next to you. The priest invites all the members of the assembly to exchange the sign of peace. According to Roman Catholic theology, the sign of peace is not transmitted in sequence from a single source. Christ, who is its only source, is present and active in the assembly. If the marriage does not take place during the celebration of Mass, the priest will omit the sign of peace. Following the sign of peace, the priest distributes Communion.

Prayer After Communion

Almighty God,
may the sacrifice we have offered
and the eucharist we have shared
strengthen the love of _____ and _____,
and give us all your fatherly aid.

(We ask this) through Christ our Lord.

Solemn Blessing

The marriage rite concludes with the recitation of the Lord's Prayer by all present followed by a solemn blessing.

God the eternal Father keep you in love with each other,
so that the peace of Christ may stay with you
and be always in your home.

Response: Amen.

May (your children bless you,)
your friends console you
and all men live in peace with you.

Response: Amen.

May you always bear witness to the love of God in this world
so that the afflicted and the needy
will find in you generous friends,
and welcome you into the joys of heaven.

Response: Amen.

And may almighty God bless you all,
the Father, and the Son, and the Holy Spirit.

Response: Amen.

To repeat, the preceding text is only an example of the assortment of prayers and readings in the Rite of Marriage. *In nearly every case there are other choices.*

A Jewish Ceremony

*T*here are only a few stipulations for a wedding to be legal under Jewish law. First the groom gives something to the bride that costs more than a dime (normally a wedding ring), and she accepts the gift. Second, the groom recites ritual words of acquisition and consecration. Third, others witness these two acts. Everything else, the participation of a rabbi, the breaking of a glass, the seven blessings, the *huppah* and the *Ketubah*, are practices that have become common in Jewish weddings, but are not requirements.

The following service is one of four services prepared by the Central Conference of American Rabbis and published in the *Rabbi's Manual* in 1988. The editor is Rabbi David Polish.

The Opening Words

The bride and groom stand under the huppah *(sometimes spelled* chupa*), a portable canopy made of fabric and held up by four poles. The rabbi speaks the words of the service first in Hebrew and next in English. Some or all of the Hebrew verses might be sung.*

Rabbi:

Blessed are you who have come here in the name of God. (We bless you in this House of God.)

Serve Adonai with joy; come into God's presence with song.

189

We rejoice that _____ and _____ join in marriage in the presence of God and loved ones.

O most awesome, glorious, and blessed God, grant Your blessings to the bride and groom.

Surrounded by loved ones whose joy and prayers are with you here, you stand at this *huppah*, symbol of the Jewish home. May your home be a shelter against the storm, a haven of peace, a stronghold of faith and love.

Let us all join in our prayer of gratitude:

We praise You, Adonai our God, Ruler of the universe, who has given us life, sustained us, and brought us to this joyous time.

Baruch Ata, Adonai Eloheinu, Melech ha-olam, shehecheyanu vekiyemanu vehigi-anu lazeman hazeh.

In this union, the sacred work of creation goes on: God joining man and woman; God planting the divine likeness within them. "Man and woman were created in the Divine image. Male and female God created them." May the union of _____ and _____ animate the Divine in each of them, and may each help the other to grow in God's likeness.

The rabbi's remarks may come here or before the Sheva Berachot (*seven marriage blessings*).

Birkat Erusin (*betrothal blessings*) *might be read here.*

Drinking from the Kiddush Cup (Betrothal Cup)

We praise You, Adonai our God, Ruler of the universe, Creator of the fruit of the vine.

The bride and groom drink from the kiddush *cup.*

We praise You, Adonai our God, Ruler of the universe, who hallows us with *mitzvot* and consecrates this marriage. We praise You, Adonai our God, who sanctifies our people Israel through *kiddushin*, the sacred rite of marriage at the *huppah*.

The Question of Intent

And now I ask you, in the presence of God and this assembly:

Do you, _____, take _____ to be your wife, to love, to honor, and to cherish?

And do you, _____, take _____ to be your husband, to love, to honor, and to cherish?

The Rings

_____ and _____, speak the words and exchange the rings that make you husband and wife.

_____, as you place the ring on the finger of the one you love, recite the words that formally unite you in marriage.

The bride and groom face each other and say successively:

Be consecrated to me with this ring as my wife in keeping with the heritage of Moses and Israel.

Be consecrated to me with this ring as my husband in keeping with the heritage of Moses and Israel.

or

Be wedded to me with this ring as my wife in keeping with the religion of the Jewish People.

Be wedded to me with this ring as my husband in keeping with the religion of the Jewish People.

The Vows

Traditionally, there are no wedding vows in a Jewish wedding. However, a bride and groom might each say these words:

Groom:

I betroth you to me forever; I betroth you to me with steadfast love and compassion; I betroth you to me in faithfulness.

Hosea 2:21–22

Bride:

I betroth you to me forever; I betroth you to me with steadfast love and compassion; I betroth you to me in faithfulness.

Hosea 2:21–22

The Blessings

Rabbi:

We praise You, Adonai our God, who hallows our people Israel through this sacred rite at the *huppah*.

Sheva Berachot
(Seven Marriage Blessings)

Rabbi (lifting cup):

We praise You, Adonai our God, Ruler of the universe, Creator of the fruit of the vine.

We praise You, Adonai our God, Ruler of the universe, Creator of all things for Your glory.

We praise You, Adonai our God, Ruler of the universe, Creator of man and woman.

We praise You, Adonai our God, Ruler of the universe, who creates us to share with You in life's everlasting renewal.

We praise You, Adonai our God, who causes Zion to rejoice in her children's happy return.

We praise you, Adonai our God, who causes bride and groom to rejoice. May these loving companions rejoice as have Your creatures since the days of creation.

Rabbi or assembly:

We praise You, Adonai our God, Ruler of the universe, Creator of joy and gladness, bride and groom, love and kinship, peace and friendship. O God, may there always be heard in the cities of Israel and in the streets of Jerusalem: the sounds of joy and of happiness, the voice of the groom and the voice of the bride, the shouts of young people celebrating, and the songs of children at play. We praise You, our God, who causes the bride and groom to rejoice together.

The groom and bride drink from the kiddush *cup.*

Rabbi:

As you have shared the wine from a single cup, so may you, under God's guidance, share contentment, peace, and fulfillment from the cup of life. May you find life's joys heightened, its bitterness sweetened, and each of its moments hallowed by true companionship and love.

The rabbi might read the Ketubah (*marriage contract*) *here.*

The Declaration

In the presence of these witnesses and in keeping with our tradition, you have spoken the words and performed the rites that unite your lives.

_____ and _____, you are now husband and wife in the sight of God, the Jewish community, and all people. I ask you and all who are gathered here to pray in silence, seeking God's blessings upon your marriage and your home.

Silent prayer.

Closing Words

Rabbi:

May God bless you and keep you.
May God's presence shine upon you
and be gracious to you.
May God's presence be with you and
give you peace.

The glass is broken.

A Civil Ceremony

Officiant:

We are gathered to unite the two of you in marriage, which is an institution ordained by the state and made honorable by the faithful keeping of good men and women in all ages, and is not to be entered into lightly or unadvisedly.

Groom:

Do you, _____ take _____ to be your wife, to love, comfort, and cherish from this day forth?

Bride:

Do you, _____ take _____ to be your husband, to love, comfort, and cherish from this day forth?

Exchange rings.

Having thus pledged yourselves each to the other, I do now, by virtue of the authority vested in me by the state(s) of _____ [state] _____ pronounce you husband and wife.

Other Useful Books

Arisian, Khoren. *The New Wedding: Creating Your Own Marriage Ceremony.* New York: Vintage Books, 1973. A collection of eleven nontraditional wedding services gathered by a Unitarian Universalist minister.

Braaten, John M. *Together, Till Death Us Do Part: Twenty-one Wedding Meditations.* C.S.S. Publishing Co., Inc., 1987. This is a collection of Protestant opening words (also called wedding sermons, wedding homilies or wedding meditations). The author is an ordained minister in the American Lutheran Church.

Brill, Mordecai; Halpin, Marlene; and Genné, William H. *Write Your Own Wedding, Revised and Updated.* Piscataway, N.J.: New Century Publishers, Inc., 1985, 1979, 1973. Contains examples of traditional and contemporary Jewish, Roman Catholic and Protestant services.

Butler, Becky. *Ceremonies of the Heart, Celebrating Lesbian Unions.* Seattle: The Seal Press, 1990. This collection includes stories about lesbian relationships and texts of the ceremonies celebrating these relationships, often called services of holy union.

Champlin, Joseph M. *Together for Life: A Preparation for Marriage and for the Ceremony.* Notre Dame, Ind.: Ave Maria Press, 1970. A marriage preparation book for Roman Catholics.

Diamant, Anita. *The New Jewish Wedding.* New York: Summit Books, 1985. An outstanding guide to Jewish wedding practices.

Eklof, Barbara. *With These Words . . . I Thee Wed.* Boston: Bob Adams, Inc., 1989. A collection of different wedding vows. Some are secular (they do not contain references to God), and some are religious (they do contain references to God). There is also advice on how to write your own vows.

Glusker, David, and Misner, Peter. *Words for Your Wedding: The Wedding Service Book.* San Francisco: Harper & Row Publishers, 1986. A collection of the standard texts from several mainline Protestant wedding services: United Church of Christ, United Methodist Church, American Lutheran Church, Episcopal Church and the United Church of Canada.

Gray, Winifred. *You and Your Wedding, Revised Edition.* New York: Bantam Books Inc., 1985, 1965, 1959. This book gives detailed information about traditional wedding etiquette.

Gruen, Yetta Fisher. *Your Wedding, Making It Perfect.* New York: Viking Penguin Inc., 1986. More detailed information about wedding etiquette.

Hass, Robert, and Mitchell, Stephen. *Into the Garden: A Wedding Anthology.* New York: HarperCollins Publishers, Inc., 1993. One hundred and eleven readings on love and marriage, plus six ceremonies.

Johnson, David. *To Love Honor and Shave Twice a Week.* Brookline, Mass.: Philomath Press, 1989. Eighteen contemporary wedding services by a Unitarian Universalist minister.

Kehret, Peg. *Wedding Vows, How to Express Your Love in Your Own Words.* Colorado Springs: Meriwether Publishing Ltd., 1989. Forty examples of vows, eleven examples of the exchange of rings and six examples of how to include family members in the service. Includes advice about how to write your own vows.

King, Horace Brown. *Together in Trust: Twenty-four Select Wedding Meditations.* C.S.S. Publishing Co., Inc., 1989. A collection of opening words, also called wedding sermons, wedding homilies or wedding meditations. All are for Protestant weddings.

Kingma, Daphne Rose. *Weddings from the Heart: Ceremonies for an Unforgettable Wedding.* Berkeley, Cal.: Conari Press, 1991. Five contemporary secular ceremonies, along with additional ideas for "ceremonial flourishes" and vows.

Klausner, Abraham J. *Weddings: A Complete Guide to All Religious & Interfaith Marriage Services.* New York: A Signet Book, New American Library, 1988. Wedding etiquette and examples of what to expect in traditional Protestant, Catholic, Jewish and Interfaith services.

Knight, George W. *Wedding Ceremony Idea Book.* Brentwood, Tenn.: JM Productions, 1984. A book designed to help Protestant couples customize their own ceremonies. The author intends the services to be upbeat and contemporary and simultaneously consistent with Protestant teachings about marriage.

Lamont, Corliss. *A Humanist Wedding Service.* Buffalo: Prometheus Books, 1972. One wedding service, with sixteen suggested readings. The service

stresses equality between men and women, reason as a guide and the importance of family. There are no references to God.

Munro, Eleanor. *Wedding Readings, Centuries of Writing and Rituals for Love and Marriage.* New York: Viking Penguin, 1989. Hundreds of readings about love and relationships. The back of the book contains a list of suggested readings for various members of the wedding party. The book's index will point you to African, Aztec, Buddhist, Chinese, Eskimo, Greek, Hebrew, Hindu, Irish, Japanese and Native American readings.

Peterson, Robert J. *A Marriage Service for You.* C.S.S. Publishing Co., Inc., 1977. A book about Christian wedding services, with examples from Episcopal, Methodist, Presbyterian, Lutheran, and Roman Catholic services.

Porter, Valerie. *The Guinness Book of Marriage.* Middlesex, Great Britain: Guinness Publishing Ltd., 1991. Amusing trivia about weddings.

Roses, Rings, and Rejoicing: An Anthology of Selected Wedding Meditations From Parish Pastors. C.S.S. Publishing Co., Inc., 1990. A collection of Protestant wedding opening words gathered by the editorial staff of C.S.S. Publishing.

Rubinstein, Helge, ed. *The Oxford Book of Marriage.* Oxford: Oxford University Press, 1990. Hundreds of readings about marriage and relationships, including a quotation from a Las Vegas justice of the peace recalling the time he married sixty-seven couples in one night: "I got it down from five to three minutes . . . I could've married them *en masse*, but they're people, not cattle. People expect more when they get married." Some readings are appropriate for weddings.

Seaburg, Carl, ed. *Great Occasions, Readings for the Celebration of Birth, Coming-of-Age, Marriage, and Death.* Boston: Beacon Press, 1968. Many of the 109 readings on marriage are suited to be read at weddings. In case things don't work out, the editor has included a "Ceremony of Divorce" in the appendix.

Stein, Molly K., and Graham, William C. *The Catholic Wedding Book.* Mahwah, N.J.: Paulist Press, 1988. Wedding etiquette for Roman Catholics, and detailed information about the Roman Catholic ritual. The authors have a delightful sense of humor.

Tessina, Tina. "Commitment, Ceremonies, Marriage and Legal Issues," *Gay Relationships for Men and Women*. Los Angeles: Jeremy P. Tarcher, Inc., 1989. An example of a holy union service for gay men and women used by a minister of the Metropolitan Community Church.

Uhrig, Larry. *The Two of Us: Affirming, Celebrating and Symbolizing Gay and Lesbian Relationships*. Boston: Altson Publications, Inc., 1984. Examples of holy union ceremonies.

Acknowledgments

I have tried to trace the ownership of all copyrighted material. If I have made any infringement, I offer my apology. On receiving notification, I will be happy to make proper acknowledgments in future editions of this book. I wish to express my thanks to all the writers and owners of copyrighted material for permissions generously extended, and especially to those who have allowed alterations and adaptations. I also wish to express my thanks to my wife, Rev. Leslie Westbrook, for her editing skills, advice and encouragement. Without her support this book would not have been possible. When no name appears following a selection, I am the author.

Roger Fritts

Sincere thanks are due to the following individuals for permission to use their writings:

Carla Amato	Margaret A. Keip
Michael Barlow-Sparkman	Paul E. Killinger
Raymond J. Baugham	Paul L'Herrou
Laurinda Bilyeu	Eugene Lipman
Gustav Buchdahl	Stephen Martz
John Corrado	Bernard H. Mehlman
Robin Colpitts Friedman	Judith L. Moore
David Friedman	Rudolph W. Nemser
Kendyl Gibbons	Kenneth L. Patton
Gordon D. Gibson	Kenneth W. Phifer
David Hostetter	Betty Pingel
James D. Hunt	Michael A. Schuler
David H. Hunter	Laurel S. Sheridan
David A. Johnson	Angeline E. M. Theisen
Joan Kahn-Schneider	Richard W. Thomas
Fred F. Keip	Stephen Weiser

Acknowledgments

Thanks to the following publishers, organizations or individuals holding copyright on the selections specified, for permission to reprint:

Selections from the English translation of the *Rite of Marriage* are copyrighted © 1969 by the International Committee on English in the Liturgy, Inc. All rights reserved.

Selections from the *Rabbi's Manual* are copyrighted © 1988 by the Central Conference of American Rabbis.

Selections from the *New Revised Standard Version Bible* are copyrighted © 1989 by the Division of Christian Education of the National Council of the Churches of Christ.

The selection from *The Prophet* by Kahlil Gibran is copyrighted © 1923 by Kahlil Gibran and renewed 1951 by Administrators C.T.A. of Kahlil Gibran Estate and Mary G. Gibran. Reprinted by permission of Alfred A. Knopf, Inc.

The selection "Love is sensing the other as a presence," is from *Inscape*, by Ross Snyder. Copyright ©1968 by Abingdon Press. Poem adapted by permission.

Excerpt from *To Have or To Be?* by Erich Fromm. Copyright ©1976 by Erich Fromm. Reprinted by permission of HarperCollins Publishers.

Excerpt from "Poetry and Marriage" from *Standing by Words*. Copyright ©1983 by Wendell Berry. Published by North Point Press and reprinted by permission of Farrar, Straus & Giroux, Inc.

"i like my body when it is with your" is reprinted from *Tulips & Chimneys* by E.E. Cummings; Edited by George James Firmage, by permission of Liveright Publishing Corporation. Copyright 1923, 1925 and renewed 1951, 1953 by E.E. Cummings. Copyright ©1973, 1976 by the Trustees for the E.E. Cummings Trust. Copyright ©1973, 1976 by George James Firmage.

The sonnet by Arthur Davison Ficke is from *Voices*, Summer 1945, and is reprinted in *A Humanist Wedding Service* by Corliss Lamont, copyrighted © 1972, Prometheus Books.

The selection from *Gift from the Sea* by Anne Morrow Lindbergh is copyrighted © 1955 by Anne Morrow Lindbergh. Reprinted by permission of Pantheon Books, a division of Random House, Inc.

The selection "Two Trees" by Janet Miles is reprinted from *Images, Women in Transition*, compiled by Janice Grana (Winona, Minnesota: Saint Mary's Press, 1991). Used by permission of the publisher. All rights reserved.

Acknowledgments

The selection from *Letters to a Young Poet* by Rainer Maria Rilke, translated by M. D. Herter Norton is copyrighted © 1934 by W. W. Norton & Company, Inc. Copyright renewed 1962 by M. D. Herter Norton. Revised edition copyright © 1954 by W. W. Norton & Company, Inc. Copyright renewed 1982 by M. D. Herter Norton.

The selection "A Credo for My Relationships" is copyrighted © 1977 by Dr. Thomas Gordon.

Selections identified as *Book of Worship* are adapted from *Book of Worship United Church of Christ*, copyrighted © 1986 by Office for Church Life and Leadership, United Church of Christ and are used by permission.

Excerpt from "The Country of Marriage" from *The Country of Marriage*, copyright © 1973 by Wendell Berry, reprinted by permission of Harcourt Brace & Company.

Excerpts from *The Jerusalem Bible* are copyrighted © 1966 by Darton, Longman & Todd, Ltd., and Doubleday, a division of Bantam Doubleday Dell Publishing Group, Inc. Reprinted by permission.

The selections from the Order of Mass from *The Roman Missal* are copyrighted © 1973 by International Committee on English in the Liturgy, Inc.